CW00825636

PENGU

AMRIT

Uma Trilok holds a doctorate degree in Education Management and has been associated with several academic institutions. She writes both in English and Hindi and her published work includes *Teesra Bindu*, *Of Autumn Roses*, *Khayalon Ke Saaye* and *The Mindscape*. She has also rendered a selection of her poetry, in her own voice, in an audio cassette.

Praise for Uma Trilok

You have done well to record Amrita-Imroz aclaimably, it will go down in the Punjabi literature and become legendary. Imroz has kept Amrita alive. What more can a woman ask for, from her lover.

—Khushwant Singh,
New Delhi

It is remarkable reading. Your sensitive approach to their sensitive relationship has been highlighted appropriately and honest confessions by Imroz have brought out the unknown part of Amrita. My congratulations.

—Kanhaiya Lal Nandan

Amrita-Imroz

A Love Story

UMA TRILOK

PENGUIN BOOKS
An imprint of Penguin Random House

PENGUIN BOOKS

USA | Canada | UK | Ireland | Australia
New Zealand | India | South Africa | China

Penguin Books is part of the Penguin Random House group of companies whose addresses can be found at global.penguinrandomhouse.com

Published by Penguin Random House India Pvt. Ltd
4th Floor, Capital Tower 1, MG Road,
Gurugram 122 002, Haryana, India

Penguin Random House India

First published by Penguin Books India 2006

Text copyright © Uma Trilok 2006
Paintings and photographs copyright © Imroz 2006
All the paintings reproduced in this book are by Imroz.

All rights reserved

10 9 8 7 6 5 4 3 2

ISBN 9780143100447

Typeset in Sabon by Mantra Virtual Services, New Delhi
Printed at Manipal Technologies Limited, India

This book is sold subject to the condition that it shall not, by way of trade or otherwise, be lent, resold, hired out, or otherwise circulated without the publisher's prior consent in any form of binding or cover other than that in which it is published and without a similar condition including this condition being imposed on the subsequent purchaser.

www.penguin.co.in

FSC www.fsc.org MIX Paper from responsible sources FSC® C043100

Foreword

Dr Uma Trilok's original book—*Amrita–Imroz: A Love Story*—begins as an expression of the author's love and regard for Amrita but further deals with Amrita and Imroz's relationship, society's strong reaction against it, the demands of the family, the price asked and the profound impact it had on Amrita's creativity.

Uma Trilok has not only recognized and understood deeply Amrita and Imroz's relationship but has also tried to present to the reader, a genuine picture of the various intricate facets of their lives, many a time using their own words.

From the time of Heer, from the time of the Vedas and Upanishads, from the time of Gargi to today, many women have desired to live their lives on their own terms and those who dared were either defeated or perished. The end was painful. We only know of Gargi's name, none of her creations have reached us. And Heer—she had to take poison.

Today's woman dreams that she be not expected only to play the role assigned to her but be left alone to live her own life in her own way. But her bitter circumstantial compulsions and the lack of courage and spirit forbids her from doing so. Her dreams remain dreams. Though she seeks her fulfilment in the lives of people such as Amrita and Imroz.

Rooted in tradition, Amrita herself sometimes was perplexed by the revolt she committed and started finding reasons and explanations in her palm lines, her zodiac sign or her previous life connections.

About sixty–sixty-five years ago, during Amrita–Imroz's youth, such live-in relationships invited strong social reactions. But, today's women like Uma Trilok can openly appreciate Amrita–Imroz's non-conformist relationship without facing the displeasure of their own families.

So far, whatever has been written about Amrita, her life style, her writing style, her creativity, her qualifications, the subject matter of her writing and the value system behind it, only a very slight mention of Imroz has been made. What he thinks of this relationship and how much he values it, has not been touched upon.

Uma Trilok, in her book, has taken Imroz along in Amrita's literary journey and has tried to assess how Imroz lived out this relationship with total commitment. People may say whatever they like but Imroz is not repentant over his decision. Whatever he may have lost or gained, he has no regrets. To resign to the will of his beloved is his joy and not his compulsion. Somewhere inside, he has risen from the materialistic to the spiritual—real and true—from *ishke majazi* to *ishke haqeeqee*, which Uma Trilok has captured during her various conversations with him.

Since this book is originally in English, it will reach a broader circle of readers. More than only for Amrita, this book will become in history, a witness to Amrita and Imroz's relationship.

Dr Dalip Kaur Tiwana,
Head, Department of Punjabi,
Punjabi University, Patiala, Punjab

Gulzar

اللہ کی گواہی، پیغمبر دے، تو پیغمبر کا گواہ کون؟

امرتا جی اپنے آپ میں بہت بڑی لیجینڈ ہیں۔ پنجابی شاعری میں، بٹوارے کے بعد کی آدھی صدی کی نمائندہ شاعرہ ہیں۔ شاعری کے علاوہ، دوپٹے کی ایک گٹھا میں ناول اور افسانے باندھ کر، وہ بھی کندھوں پر پھینک لیا ہے۔ اور محبت کا ایک ایسا دوشالہ اوڑھ لیا ہے جو امروز کی 'بگھ' سے مہکتا رہتا ہے۔ اب کون بتائے کہ دوشالے نے انہیں لپیٹ رکھا ہے، یا وہ دوشالے کو 'چنچھی نمارے' رہتی ہیں۔

امروز، ایک اور لیجینڈ ہے جو پہلے اندرجیت کے نام سے روشن تھا۔ اس کے شمع کے سر ورق (cover pages) دیکھ کر لوگوں نے اس قلم اور ٹرسی کی پرستش شروع کر دی تھی جس سے ڈرائنگ کیا کرتا تھا۔ میں اس زمانے میں ملا تھا اسے! لیکن اس نے، اس روشنی کو امرتا جی کی دوستی اور محبت میں یوں تحلیل کر دیا کہ ایک اور چراغ جلا، ان دونوں کی دوستی کا۔ اب وہ دوستی اپنے آپ میں تیسرا لیجینڈ ہے.... مرحبا!

ان کا رشتہ نظم اور امیج کا رشتہ ہے۔ آپ بتا نہیں سکتے، کہ تخلیق کے جنم کے لئے، کس نے پہل کی۔ نظم ہوئی تو امیج بنی، یا امیج آئی تو نظم ہوئی۔ امرتا جی کی نظمیں پینٹنگز کی طرح خوش رنگ ہیں۔ وہ ورد کی آواز ہوں یاد لاسے کی۔ اسی طرح امروز کی پینٹنگز نظموں کے آب حیات پر تیرتی ہیں۔

گلزار
8.2.2005

"BOSKYANA", PALI HILL, BANDRA (W), MUMBAI - 400 050 TEL. OFF 2646 1957, 2649 8351, FAX 2604 0477

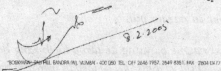

Allah ki gawahi Paigumbar de to Paigumbar ka gawah kaun?

Amritaji apne aap mein ek bari legend *hain.*
Punjabi shayari mein batware ke baad ki aadhi sadi ki numainda shayara hain.
Shayari ke ilawa dupatte ki ek githa mein novel *aur afsane bandh kar voh bhi kandho par faink liya hai, aur mohabat ka ek aisa dushala oarh liya hai, jo Imroz ki nigh se mehakta rehata hai. Ab kaun bataye ke dushale ne unhe lapet rakha hai, ya voh dushale ko japhee mare rehti hain.*

Imroz ek aur legend *hai, jo pehle Inderjeet ke naam se roshan tha. Us ke sarvark dekh kar logon ne us kalam aur kursi ki parstish shuru kar di jis se* drawing *kiya karta tha. Mai us zamane mein mila tha use. Lekin usne us roshni ko Amrita ji ki dosti aur mohabat main yoon tehleel kar diya ki ek aur chirag jala—un dono ki dosti ka.*

Ab vho dosti apne aap mei tesra legend *hai . . . Marhaba*

Un ka rishta nzam aur image *ka rishta hai.*
Aap bata nahi sakte ke takhlique ke janam ke liye kis ne pehel ki.
Nazam hui to image *bani.*
Ya
Image *aayee to nazam hui.*

Amrita ji ki nazme painting *ke tarha kush rang hai. Voh dard ki aavaz hon ya dilase ki. Isi tarhan Imroz ki* paintings *nazmo ke aabohyat par tairti hain.*

Boskiyana,
Mumbai.

Gulzar

. . . Sojourns

Sometimes, occasionally, purposefully or whenever I met Amrita and Imroz. I was touched by their togetherness, their being for each other, their friendship, their sharing, their unpronounced unexpressed love for each other. A kind of a humming of a song, I experienced, which seemed very valuable to me. I must have desired to store it and hide it in my heart.

Those experiences, I have tried to put on paper.

This book is not like any other book. It is neither based on any research, nor does it have any structured or systematized style. It is a random collection of annotations about two unconventional people—their undefined love and friendship.

In a way, this is a brief interactive portrayal of my decade old friendship with Amrita and Imroz. Whenever they touched my life and what ever gushed out of that experience, I have tried to put it on paper.

It may also be seen as an expression or a short collection of indulgent smiles, hearty laughter, physical suffering, emotional agony, social defiance and some more.

It is a book about an author and an artist.

An author who stirred the very core of Punjab and beyond, by her powerful writings, recitations and her lifestyle, and an artist who has painted the very soul of their relationship from different perspectives.

To write about such a great writer and poet, and her friend who is the focus of her life, needs the creative expertise of the same standard, which I do not posses. My only qualification is that, in my own humble way, I have known Amrita and Imroz as friends, by virtue of which I got a chance to know and observe their emotional selves closely.

No doubt the book suffers from many shortcomings, but I have tried to be as honest as I could be, notwithstanding my highest respect for both of them.

Amrita for me is an enigmatic mixture of my childhood adorations, which has developed into friendship and deep respect. I have experienced her—as a friend, as a guide, as a writer, as a mentor, as a poet and much, much more . . . as my little baby.

Directly and indirectly this collection has been made possible by the persuasion, efforts and cooperation of many people over a long period of time.

I am very grateful to my reiki gurus—Reiki Masters Dr Nalin Nirula and Mrs Renoo Nirula who very warmly responded to my request to visit Amrita ji, when I felt that my treatment of Amritaji needed their support. Renooji visited her often and also guided and encouraged me to provide appropriate treatment and care to Amritaji.

The book is a result of the constant urging, coaxing and help from Saumya—my daughter, who despite the preoccupation with her doctoral studies, found time to read and discuss progressive versions of the manuscript. Trilok, my husband helped me with corrections and review of the book.

I am also grateful to my poet and writer friends—Taranum Ryaz, Rakshat Puri, Inder Batra 'Sahil', Jaipal Nangia for their valuable inputs, and Amit Bhatia, CEO, of A'N'B Communications Ltd, for his encouragement and guidance.

However, the person who made it all possible is Imroz.

He had once said:

Rab ne bande banaye han
Te bandeyan ne dostiyan aap banaiyian han
Meri te Amrita dohan dee Uma dost hai
Saade nazdeek dost oh hai
Jis dee presence vee asi enjoy karde haan
Saadi gal baat te, sun sunaan da silsila
Chalda rehnda hai—telephone te ve,e te mil ke vee
Dosti da vee ik darya hunda hai
Jo Dostan nu zerkhez karda renda hai

(God created people and people themselves made friendships.
Uma is a friend of ours—Amrita's and mine.
For us a close friend is one, whose presence we enjoy.
With her our communication continues—in person as well as on the phone.
Friendship for us is like river water,
Which continuously nourishes and strengthens the bonds among friends.)

With his open-book approach to life, he smilingly shared his feelings and experiences along with cups of tea, which he often prepared himself. He took time to explain his paintings to me. Even when I hesitatingly asked him some personal questions he answered them unhesitatingly. He also very graciously allowed me to include some of his paintings in this book.

Thank you Imroz.

And how does one thank a friend like Amrita—originally my Amritaji . . .

I am very grateful to both of them for accepting me as a friend.

I am especially grateful to Gulzarji—a legend himself, for introducing the other two legends—Amrita and Imroz.

I am grateful to God for giving me a chance to meet and interact with two individuals who lived a unique life of love and friendship.

Uma Trilok

One

In 1996, on my way from Dehra Dun to Delhi, I had picked up Amrita Pritam's new book of poems 'Sometimes I Tell this Tale to the River', translated by Arlene Zide. I read it uninterrupted. I was gripped by her words. Some of her expressions like—*begging for a pinch of that musk* and *sun asking for an ember to kindle his fire*, from her poem 'Early Spring' touched an inner chord.

Words from another poem 'Window'—*time got bruised and bled*—elevated me to some other time zone. Her poem 'A Meeting' created an euphoria—a kind of madness that does not belong to this world. She writes:

We met at daybreak
Like torn pieces of a sheet of paper
I grasped his hand in mine
He clasped me in his arms

Then again, like censors
We both laughed
We put that sheet of paper on the cold table
And crossed out the entire poem.

In another poem, she says: 'History came to my kitchen and went away hungry.' She also goes on to portray her experiences with the strokes of a painter's brush—'Time that swept away the smouldering coals of her life and got blisters on its fingertips.' I felt mystified by her impudence and imagery. As I turned each page I could feel the presence of the author around me. My desire to have a personal meeting with her became an obsession by the time I reached the end of the book.

In Delhi, I was in search of Amritaji. I was in constant search of a person who could guide me or link me to her.

During a cultural meet at the India International Centre, I met an author friend of hers. I requested him to introduce me to her. 'She does not keep well, these days. So she does not entertain visitors,' he said. However, on my insistence, he hesitatingly gave me her address and phone number.

With each day, my desire to meet her became a fixation. One day a friend suggested that I should present my recently released second book of poems, *Khayalon ke Saye*, along with an audio cassette of my poems, rendered in my own voice, to her, and seek her comments and guidance. This idea gave me an excuse and an opportunity to establish contact with her. I felt ecstatic. I waited for her to get well.

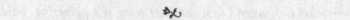

Two

I had known about Amritaji since my childhood. I had sung many songs written by her. I think I was twelve years old, when I first sang her song at a gathering. I did not understand the deep emotions expressed in her words then, but I enjoyed the lyric and the beat within. With time, her songs had found a permanent place in my heart. Every time I read any of her writings or heard her on radio or saw her on television, I felt a fresh emotional wave in my heart, creating a new bond.

I continued to sing her songs during my school and college days. Even today I can vividly recall the silence, the emotionally charged environment, and the moist eyes of the audience and tears in my own eyes, as I sang Amritaji's famous song on partition of India—'Waris Shah'. The song always ended with silence and a few sobs from the audience. The clapping, subdued and respectful, for the poem and the poet—Amrita Pritam. Her words and thoughts could make even the indifferent stop, listen, feel and think about the agony and the suffering of partition. Especially the girls.

I knew Amritaji's birthday falls on 31 August. This was an opportune time to meet her. I contacted her friend. I knew he would be visiting her. I wanted to go along with him. I persuaded him to call her, and request her for a short meeting. Amritaji agreed. I was very happy and excited. I specially dressed for the occasion. Picking up the choicest flowers from the market I got ready to meet her.

We reached her house in Hauz Khas around 11.30 in the morning. It is a three-storey building surrounded by trees all around. Potted plants and creepers decorated the walk-in corridor. A large hibiscus tree partially covered the building. It had an iron gate supported by pillars and a wall made of stones. On the right side of the gate was written the name Amrita Pritam, in very artistic handwriting, in dull ochre and yellow.

I felt excitement in my heart. Passing through the porch, we came to a wooden door painted in dull orange. On the right side of the door frame, there was a call bell. Under the bell were the names—Amrita–Imroz, written in small letters. Looking at the plants outside Amrita's house, I recalled, in one of her books Amrita had narrated a Gujarati song—'*Sayyan re tu meri gali ko chail kari pehna de*', where she imagined a locality of earthen houses covered with tiles. An area where the youth blossomed and attracted a young urbanite. Shy of her humble locale the girl asks for a favour from her lover—'*Sayyan re meri gali ko chail kari pehna de.*' In other words 'My Love, if I may ask for a favour, please plant a *chail kari* in my lane.'

As I walked towards the house, I searched for the bright green leaves and deep red flowers of '*chail kari*'. Amrita had mentioned once that she did not know when she had expressed a desire for this, or when Imroz had heard her and had planted a *'chail kari'* in the small courtyard of her house, and in all the four corners of the terrace. Now, in the evening of her life, she sometimes goes upstairs slowly, holding Imroz's hand to reach the *chail kari,* just to touch it with her lips.

Three

Amritaji lives on the first floor.

We were going up the stairs. The whole staircase was decorated with paintings by Imroz.

Moving up the staircase was a unique experience.

I found Amritaji in each painting. They differed in style and provided a different perspective of her. I wanted to spend more time with each painting, to understand and interact with the many facets of Amritaji's persona.

Imroz, the artist, had left his mark on the walls, on the lampshades and on the floor as well. The floor of the staircase was decorated with a rangoli. Amritaji was present all over, as visualized and perceived by Imroz. A concurrence of body and soul, image and reality.

Although I had not yet entered the house I experienced it as if I had already had an interface with her.

'Tukron mein mulaaquat ho gayee ho jaise.'
(A meeting in bits and pieces had already taken place.)
'Unki saundhi kushboo jaise aane lag pari ho'

(As if her earthy smell had already reached me)
'Meine unhe apne bahut kareeb paaya'
(I could feel her very close to me)
'Voh Amrita jo apne sare kirdaaron ka kuch kuch hissa thee.'
(That Amrita, who was a part of each of her characters created in her books.)

Going up the stairs, we entered a room. On the left there was the dining area. We turned to the right and passed through a large room, full of paintings and calligraphy, to reach Amritaji's bedroom. As we passed through the large room I saw a big table with a mirror on top, over which lay a large branch of a tree. I could see the artistically placed branch as well as its reflection in the mirror—an unusually beautiful sight. What was it symbolic of? I had yet to discover.

As we entered the bedroom, we saw Amritaji sitting on the edge of her bed. Although she was not well, she looked bright. I could not help staring at her face admiringly. Responding to my greetings and looking at me she smiled warmly. I felt touched by her warmth and grace. Gently placing the bouquet of flowers in her lap, I whispered a soft 'Happy Birthday'.

I saw a smiling, petite, pretty face, with a mole on one cheek, short hair, fair complexion and a delicate build. I specifically noticed her dainty hands and shapely fingers. I wondered how such a delicate person could have produced such a vast body of literature. Amrita is the first woman recipient of the Sahitya Akademi Award, winner of the most prestigious Jnanpith Award, a Padmashri, now a Padma

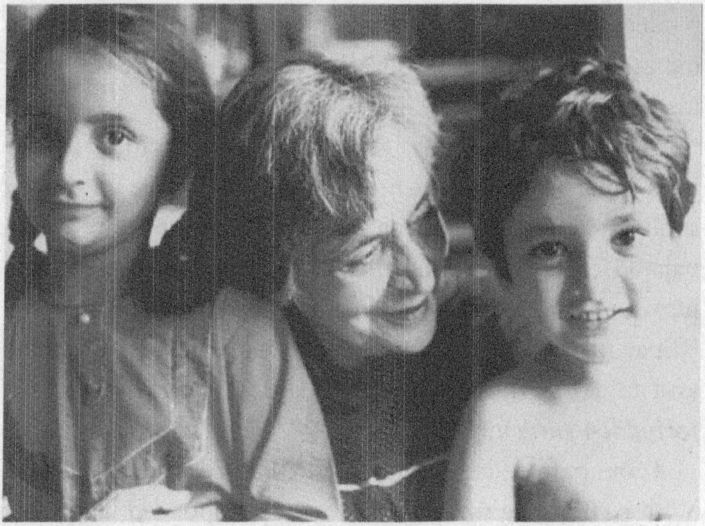

Vibhushan and an awardee of many other prestigious awards in India and abroad. Six universities have conferred D.Lit. degrees on her. She has been honoured with titles like *Awaz-e-Punjab* and has been called the 'poetess of the millennium'.

There was a very special glimmer in her brown eyes. She had a cool and content look with a calm expression on her face. There was no sign of denial or disturbance on her face. She seemed to be flowing like a river—slow and mysterious.

While I was absorbing what I had imagined and what I had not, I quickly presented my book and the audio cassette to her. She smiled again. She read out the name of my book aloud—'*Khayalon ke Saaye*'. She looked admiringly at the cover of the book and said, 'Beautiful cover. Nice name. Good blend of black and white.'

As she glanced through the book she asked, 'Have you

rendered your poems in your own voice?' Then she looked at me indulgently and said in a thoughtful way, 'It is a good idea to bring out poetry in audio cassettes.'

Hers is a very soft and gentle voice with no force or fury in it. Inner turmoil, if there was any, was hidden or already sublimated. At this moment, a tall gentleman in white kurta-pajama entered the room. Amrita's friend got up to greet him. Looking towards me he said '*Uma, yeh Imroz hain*' (Uma, this is Imroz). 'Imroz'—the name ignited my mind and my first thought was *Oh, Imroz—the hero of the forbidden garden?*

I got up, folded my hands, and mumbled a soft '*Namaste*'. With a charming smile on his face, he responded warmly to our greetings. Moving towards the door, he said: '*Ik minute ruko, main thwade layee cake lai ke ana aye*' (Wait, I will bring some cake for you.)

With a smile on his face, Imroz left the room quickly. Looking at him, I recollected Amritaji's poem '*Amb da butda*' referring to Imroz, where she says:

But tusadra amb da butda
Veh kehre bagan vich lagra
Varhan te vaali vidarn sanoo
Sanoo tan eh dukh dadra . . .

Saun ja nee malan
Saun ja ne bhaina
Amba dee raakhee virha jo baithra
Te gal vich geet sugalra

Where would you get planted, oh my Mango Sapling
People forbid me
Grief strikes me
Fenced as I am
My pain deepens . . .

You sing yourself to sleep
My friend, oh gardener
Let the anguish of separation
Be enough, to guard
(The Mango Sapling)

Imroz was her 'mango sapling'. About Imroz she had written that '. . . from the shadows of the moon, Imroz descended into the night and entered my dreams . . . one day someone brought him home.' She had also written '. . . he was a painter from Bombay and he illustrated beautifully, they said his name was Imroz. . . . I found him very silent, absolutely non-communicative, yet I felt he was speaking.'

My thoughts were interrupted. Imroz returned with the cake and started serving it.

'Today is Majaa's birthday,' he said. Imroz lovingly calls Amrita by the name Majaa.

Much later he told me why. They had both read an Italian novel in which the heroine's name was Majaa. Imroz liked the name so much that ever since that time, he had called her Majaa.

'Would you like to have some tea?' he asked.

The author friend smiled and said, 'Okay.' I consented by my silence. Imroz again returned to the kitchen to bring tea.

Amritaji and her author friend were discussing some publishers. My thoughts went back to Imroz and Amritaji.

Imroz and Amritaji have been living together for nearly forty years. Imroz surrounds her. He paints her, paints the windows of her house, illustrates her books, builds their bookcases, writes poetry on her lampshades and calligraphs her name in the form of a tree. His large painting of the tree hangs in the room near her bedroom. Imroz is an integral part of Amritaji's poetry—very vivid and very prominent. I was reminded of the following lines from her poem *Adi Dharam*:

> 'When I wrapped myself with your being
> Our bodies turned inwards in contemplation
> Our limbs intertwined
> Like blossoms in a garland
> Like an offering at the altar of the spirit . . .
> Our names, slipping out of our lips,
> Became a sacred hymn . . .

Imroz came into the room again with two cups of tea and handed them over to us. Drawing up a chair, he sat down, close to us. I observed a winsome smile on his face, expressive of a unique inner simplicity and contentment. Seeing two people so spiritually entwined together and revelling in each other's presence, I could virtually hear a sacred hymn. Everybody knows Imroz is the 'man' in Amritaji's life and Amritaji is the only person in Imroz's life. I was completely immersed in their presence.

Amritaji has lived her life on her own terms irrespective of what the world thought. She has the power and capacity to walk alone and without restraint. I was experiencing Amritaji's serenity and Imroz's fulfilment. Their attunement was similar to the first and the fifth notes of the octave.

We finished tea. Amritaji was talking about her physical ailments. Quite recently she had had an operation. I suggested naturopathy to her and asked her if she would like to consult a naturopath. She remained quiet for a while and then looked at Imroz for an answer. After a few moments of silence she said, 'Perhaps I will.' Exhaustion was evident on her face. She needed rest. We decided to leave. I gave her my visiting card and mentioned that I would arrange for an appointment with the naturopath in a day or two. She responded with a warm and charming smile. I had a deep desire to linger on. As we drove back, my mind was full of Amritaji and Imroz and his paintings.

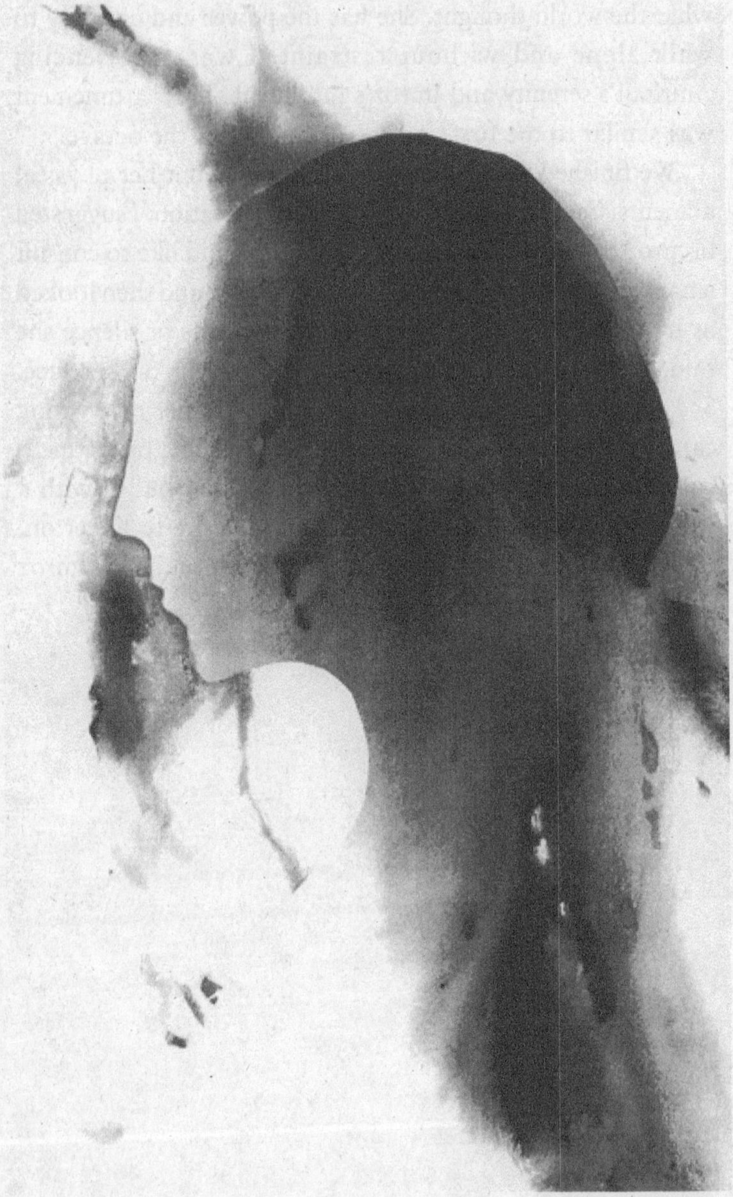

Four

Soon after returning from my meeting with Amritaji, I tried to contact the naturopath whom I had known for some time. When I called Amritaji's house to enquire about the convenient time for me to visit her house with the naturopath, she suggested that she would like to complete the current treatment and dosage and also consult her doctor.

I was looking forward to meeting Amritaji again—this time on my own. I wanted to ask her so many things; know her as a person. I also wanted to understand Imroz. Early in the morning on the fifth of September, my telephone rang. On picking up the receiver, I heard the words: *'Umaji mein Amrita bol rahi haan, tusi naturopath di gal keetee see kadon chalna chaheeda hai?'* (Uma, I am Amrita speaking, you mentioned about the naturopath, when should we see him?)

I was thrilled to hear her voice on the phone. I asked her about her convenience. She said: *'Parson savere nau ku vaje.'* (Day after tomorrow around nine in the morning.)

I said, *'Amritaji mai phir sade nau vaje dee appointment lai leni haan te main nau vajai tak tuwahade kol pahunch jaavaangee*'. (Amritaji, I will take appointment for nine-thirty and will reach your place around nine.)

This call had a very special significance for me. I was getting a chance to be with the person I had admired almost all my life. I had sung her songs, read her books, heard about her controversies, debated her thoughts in seminars and now would have a chance to interact with her in a personal and private environment. It was a special date. I had my car cleaned and checked. I made sure I had enough time for all the traffic jams and still be on time for my appointment. Just to double-check about her health and her ability to go to the naturopath, I called up at her house. Imroz told me that she was getting ready for the appointment.

When I reached their house, both Amritaji and Imroz were standing outside their house waiting for me. Amritaji was holding Imroz's hand to take support for walking. I apologized for being late. In a cheerful voice she said, 'Uma, you are not late, we are early.'

Amritaji sat in front with me and Imroz sat in the back. She was happy to be out of the house. She was feeling weak but was in good spirits. She told me how she enjoyed being in the open and expressed her concern about the increasing traffic and pollution in the city. Then she enquired about my recent work. She told me that she had enjoyed reading my poems and encouraged me to continue writing without fear or worry of criticism. She encouraged me to share my feelings freely. She also talked about her health. She was not sure if naturopathy would help her at that stage but she had faith in the principles of naturopathy.

Reflecting on her health, Amirtaji remarked that when

we are in good health we take it for granted. We understand the importance of good health only when we lose it. We never expect to ever suffer from any ill health or physical pain. For Amritaji emotional pain had been a part of the process of living. She found so much suffering and pain in her surroundings that it continued to be expressed through her writing.

Due to the office-time traffic, the drive was slow. It gave us an opportunity to talk about many things, such as other poets and writers. Her views and feelings towards Shiv Batalvi were of special interest to me. He had fascinated me for a long time.

She narrated how Batalvi had experienced agony in his life and shared it in his poems and songs. Besides many other factors pain seemed to be a common ground between the two poets. While on the subject of pain and Shiv Batalvi, I remembered what she had said about him: 'May thy pain live for ever; I know not whether it is a blessing or a curse.'

I wondered about her writings on pain. Amritaji's own relationship with pain is deep and mature. In one of her poems she says:

Whenever, wherever earth quaked
A deep sigh escaped my chest.

Amritaji's own image of herself is also full of pain and her poetry reflects this:

That was an ache
I smoked

And flicked off
A few poems as ash.

We reached the naturopath's clinic. Amritaji was anxious and wanted Imroz to come along with her to the consultation room. As he held her hand and accompanied her, I could see her anxiety disappear. I could visualize a confident lady, who had walked alone with her own set of values. She wanted Imroz to listen to the consultant's advice carefully. Again, I could see a kind of deep-rooted anxiety in her which was being taken care of by Imroz's presence. Holding his hand like a small child, she walked very slowly into the clinic. Her slow gait was a strange amalgam of past social defiance and the current reality of physical weakness. A vignette of numerous time frames, colours and shades.

I wondered how a lady who had changed the direction of the social as well as cultural streams of her times through her powerful writing could feel so helpless. I was not sure whether it was physical helplessness or emotional dependence. In some of her writings, Amritaji has suggested that her mind was always in search of someone bigger than herself, who would help give expression to her creative surge. Perhaps she found this in Imroz.

In another context she had expressed her views on love saying that there was one kind of love, like that of the sky, and there was another one, which was like a roof over one's head. Sahir Ludhianvi was 'like the sky' for her. A woman seeks both, she had said, and the roof eventually opens to the sky. It was chance and circumstance that she chose the roof. The sky was very distant. Love, for her, had immediacy, an energy that stirred her, awakened her.

As I was driving them back, she was in a more relaxed mood. She was impressed by the naturopath and expressed her desire to visit him again. She also promised to follow his instructions. On reaching her house, I walked her up to her bedroom. Imroz offered me tea and we had it in Amritaji's bedroom. As I was about to leave she said, '*Uma, tere nal mil ke mainu bari khushi hui hai. Hun tu mainu mildi reha karin.*' (Uma, I am happy to have met you, now you should continue to meet me.)

Imroz walked me out to the gate. As we crossed the big room and walked down the stairs, Imroz talked about some of his paintings on the walls of the staircase. This marked the beginning of my bond with Amritaji and Imroz.

Five

Amritaji's treatment at the nature cure centre continued for some time but her system did not respond very positively to it. I was visiting her almost every alternate day. One day in the month of January, when I was at her house she complained of acute pain in her leg and was very restless. At that time I suggested that she may like to consider Pranic healing. After discussing the nuances of Pranic healing as well as reiki, I casually mentioned to her that I was a trained Pranic healer and also a reiki channel. I told her that I had taken training in reiki from the famous reiki master Mrs Renoo Nirula.

Amritaji said that she did not know much about either of them. Looking at me smilingly she said, 'If you take me as your patient I would be willing to try. Uma, I want to get rid of my pain. Perhaps you can understand my agony.'

To initiate the Pranic healing process, I helped her get into a comfortable position on the bed. With Imroz's help, I got a bowl of water with some salt in it. As they did not have sea salt at home, I used ordinary salt. When I requested her to touch the top of her mouth with the tip of her tongue she was amused and started laughing. I gently took her hands and put them on her knees with her palms open and pointing upwards. As she got into the receptive pose for the healing, I positioned myself in front of her and proceeded with the healing.

She accepted the healing with a gentle smile on her face. I could sense a wave of restfulness and relaxation passing through her body. Soon she fell into a slumber and then moved into deep sleep. After a few softly spoken words with Imroz, I left her sleeping. Imroz walked me to the door. As we went down the stairs, Imroz said, '*Amrita taan kise nu kol nai aan dendi, twade naal taan baut ralmil gai ai.*' (Amrita does not allow anybody to come close to her, but with you she seems to mix around quite uninhibitedly.) I left with a sense of satisfaction; also a sense of gratitude towards divinity. From the next day onwards I started giving her healing.

Next day, in the morning, she called and said, '*Uma, toon te kal jaadoo kar ditta, aini pakki need te kadi aayee hee nahi, te dard vee hat gayee see, pher kado aayengee?*' (I have never slept as soundly as I slept yesterday. What magic did you do? Even the pain settled down. When will you come again?)

I said, '*Shukar hai rab da ke twanu aaraam miliya hai. Je twaanu aaraam aave taan main roz aawangee.*' (I am grateful to God for giving you relief. If you feel relieved, I will visit you every day.)

'*Tainu mil ke mainu baut changa lagda hai, te aaram vee aaya cee. Mere walon roz aaya kar.*' (I feel happy in meeting you. There is also some relief from pain. You are welcome to visit me every day.)

I could feel the warmth in her voice and a desire to meet. Two days later I visited her again. Alka, her daughter-in-law, escorted me to her bedroom. As I walked in both Amrita and Imroz greeted me with warm smiles. They were sitting together, chatting with each other, like two love birds. It was a very heart-warming sight. During our conversation she complained of sporadic spells of pain. Imroz, sitting close to her on the bed, pressed her leg gently, and consoled her.

My thoughts wandered. I recalled what she had advised Imroz in one of her books: 'You are young. This is the time for you to settle down. You go your way. As far as I am concerned, I may not live long.' He said, 'Living without you is like dying. I do not want to die.' Dejected and sad, one day again she said, 'Why don't you go and see the world first. If you return and still want to be with me I will do whatever you will want me to do.' Imroz took three rounds of her small room and said, 'Okay, now I have seen the world.'

Reminiscing, Amritaji had said, 'What does one say to a person like that? What does one do? Laugh or cry?'

I recalled that before Amritaji and Imroz started living together, she had visited an astrologer and asked him a direct question: 'Will this union take place?'

The astrologer read some lines, made some calculations and said: 'It is a union of only two-and-a-half hours.'

She got up in anger and said: 'No, this cannot be so.'

The astrologer looked at his calculations again and quickly said: 'If not for two-and-a-half hours, it may last for two-

and-a-half months or perhaps for two-and-a-half years.'

'If it is only a matter of a figure of two-and-a-half, then why not two-and-a-half lifetimes?' she had asked abruptly. 'Half of my life is over, and two lifetimes are left,' she had continued thoughtfully.

The pundit was not familiar with such intense emotional logic. She came out of the astrologer's place in a disturbed state of mind. She realized she was treading a path of turmoil. Emotionally, she had gone past the shaded trees of the Garden of Eden and was walking amidst the dry shrubs.

Some people known to her had suggested that she could

have lived with whosoever she wanted, but she did not have to injure her relationship with the world. But how could she have told them that she did not care much about the world. That she did not want to please the world. She only wanted to please her Ranjha (hero of the love epic *Heer-Ranjha*).

My thoughts continued to wander. Proving the pundit wrong, I could see Amritaji had not forgotten her words that the relationship will last two-and-a-half lifetimes. Is this the same self-will that sages talk of, when divinity bends before them and comes along as they expect it to? I wondered. To me it appeared that their relationship was not of this lifetime alone. It had a continuity—a past-life connection.

My thoughts again took a turn. For twenty years, every second or third day Amritaji would dream of a two-storey house, overlooking a forest and a river at the back of the house. Close to the window, a man stood painting on a canvas. This continued for twenty years. She had said she never saw the man's face—she only saw either his back or his profile. But when she met Imroz she recognized him instantaneously. She never saw the dream again after meeting him.

Is this what destiny is all about? I wondered.

Six

What the world calls an act of blasphemy, Amrita has committed it boldly. She has expressed it in her poems, and she has lived it.

Today I have sold a world
And bought a world of beliefs.

I committed an act of blasphemy
I wove a bolt of dreams
Tore off a yard
And sewed a blouse for my life.

In ordinary terms Amrita committed not only an act of blasphemy but also something more than that. Even though she was a married woman she lived with another man whom she loved and who loved her—but without any social sanction. Amrita and Imroz have both vehemently denied their need for any social endorsement.

Once when I specifically asked Imroz this question he said,

'Couples who are not sure of their love for each other need social sanction. We know our minds well, so where was there any need of any social intervention? In our case society had no role to play.' He added pointedly, 'Why do we have to commit before society that we are committed to each other? If you are committed, or if you are not, society cannot help you in any case. We expect the society to take a decision for us or put a stamp of approval on our decision, only when we don't want to exercise our own free will and do not take responsibility of our own actions.

'When we take our own decisions ourselves, we cannot blame others for whatever wrong that may come on us,' he continued. 'It is here that we want to play safe and bring society in, for our own convenience. Amrita and I did not need that convenience.'

Interrupting him, I asked Amritaji, 'Don't you think you have broken a social norm and have set a bad example?'

She kept quiet for a while and then, with several gaps of silence, as if talking to herself, went on, 'No. I feel we both have strengthened this relationship of love. Love is the very basis of marriage. How have we broken a social norm? *Ham ne tan, man, karan aue vachen se nibhaya hai jo shayed doosre jore nehin kar paaye hain. Ham ne har mushkil ka saamna kiya hai ikathe. Aur har sachaayee se yeh rishta jiya hai.'* (We have been loyal and sincere to each other through body, mind, action and word. Which perhaps other couples have not. We have faced every problem together and have sustained this relationship in complete truthfulness.)

She unhesitatingly and proudly continued, 'In fact we have put forth a very strong and effective example before society.

We have in fact strengthened society. Why should we feel shy or ashamed; in fact they should be ashamed for misjudging us.'

As a writer, Amritaji had had to suffer a lot of opposition. People opposed her because of her free and frank style of writing and her own unconventional personal lifestyle. But wagging tongues never bothered her. Before she separated from her husband she had encouraged him to face the truth boldly; to accept the fact that they both needed to go their own individual ways separately and not be afraid of people's scorn or criticism. She believes that one needs the courage to face the truth.

A noted Hindi writer had once asked her that if all the heroines of her novels left their homes in search of truth wouldn't its effect be shattering in the context of society? Amrita had composedly replied that if false social values accounted for broken homes, more homes should be broken on the altar of truth.

I was beginning to experience the magic of Amritaji's courageous and multifaceted persona.

Seven

My visits to Amritaji's house became more frequent. She had started responding to Pranic healing. She was feeling much better. She was more cheerful and was able to cope with the pain. She would often say, *'Hun toon naaga na paya kar. Rozana aaya kar.'* (Now, don't skip a day. Come daily.)

Our healing sessions continued quite regularly. Sometimes she would say: *'Hun mainu swaad aan lag paya hai.'* (Now I have started enjoying the therapy.) However, because she had visitors, we had to skip a few healing sessions. Also, during this time, my daughter Saumya, who was a student at the London School of Economics (LSE), came to visit us and I was spending most of my time with her.

One day, early in the morning, I received a call from her. As I picked up the phone she said:*'Meri ek dost hundi see jeeda naam Uma see, ohnoo kayeen oh mainu kiyoon bhul gayee hai. Ohnoo kayeen mainu milan te aave.'* (I had a friend whose name was Uma. Ask her why she has forgotten me. Tell her to come and meet me sometimes.)

With a smile in my voice, I said *'Mein jaldi aawangee ma'am.'* (I will come soon ma'am.)

The same afternoon I went to visit her. She was feeling weak and was resting at that time. As soon I touched her forehead she woke up.

I enquired, 'How are you ma'am'?

She said, 'Please don't call me ma'am or Amritaji. Just call me Amrita. *Ham dost hain.'* (We are friends.)

I said, 'No ma'am, you are my guru.'

She replied, *'Nahin main kise dee guru nahin. Teri taan bilkul nahi.'* (I am nobody's guru; least of all yours.)

'*Achchha*, then you are my little baby,' I said.

She started laughing, '*Haan eh theek hai.*' (Yes, that is all right.) I would like to be your little baby,' she said, smiling like a baby.

The one-time literary lioness of Punjab looked so vulnerable, so helpless and also so sweet that I felt like picking her up in my arms like a little baby.

Sometimes, suddenly, like a baby, she would say, 'My leg is giving me a lot of pain. Can't your Pranic healing or reiki healing do something about it soon?'

I would laugh and reply, 'Why not? Let us do something about it.'

As soon as I started giving her healing, she would become restful. Often she would go to sleep. And sometimes, holding my hand, she would start sharing her thoughts and would reminisce. She would sometimes ask, 'What do you do with your hands that I start feeling better?'

I would simply laugh. She liked to have her leg massaged. Often she would ask Imroz to press her leg, which he would gladly and promptly do. She would frequently call out to Imroz (she lovingly calls him Ima) and say, *'Ima lat daba de, bahut peer hai.'* (Ima please press my leg, I am having pain.)

That day Amrita was in a questioning mood. 'When we have to die, why do we have to suffer pain?' she asked. 'Why do we linger on with so much pain?'

'Yes, to die of nothingness is easier than to die of pain,' I wanted to say.

'Why don't we just die?' she asked.

In my naive way, I put forward a traditional answer, 'Pain purifies us.'

She simply smiled and said, 'But with pain we become vulnerable, we lose our privacy. Perhaps it purifies us also, in the sense that we can empathize better with those who are in pain.' She started reciting her poem:

Rooh da ik zakham
Bara aam rog hai
Zakham de nangez ton
Je bahut sharam aave
Te sapne da tota parh ke
Oh zakham utte laa lave.
(The soul gets wounded often; to save it from shame a scrap of dream may be used to cover the naked wounds.)

While listening to her poems and reminiscences, I continued to give her healing and she went into a slumber reciting her poem softly. While she was sleeping, sitting by her side, I remembered how once she had talked about the 'pain of creation'. She had said, 'Uma, you must be knowing about

Kunti, the character from the Mahabharata. She was gifted to call any god to fulfil a wish. Kunti called the Sun God, which resulted in the birth of her illegitimate son Karan from the Sun God. Kunti had to abandon her son for fear of society. She was unprotected, absolutely alone and helpless. You know, that kind of situation gives rise to a "pain of creation"'

How well she understood Kunti's compulsions and her acute pain that arose out of it. I quietly left her bedside.

Eight

Early one morning my phone rang. When I picked up the receiver, Amrita said, *'Amrita bol rahi haan, ki haal ai?'* (I am Amrita speaking, how are you?') Before I could answer, she continued: *'Uma, Aainiyan sohniyaan nazma likhdee hain aur dasdi vee nahin. Aj savere paryaan, do ku nazma taan meri rooh vich hee khub gayeean, hein.'* (You write such beautiful poems and never even talk about them. I read them in the morning today. A few of them have virtually pierced through my soul.)

Hearing these words I became very emotional. I could feel tears choking my throat. I could hardly talk but I tried to, and she must have heard the tears in my voice. For a while, she was quiet and then very warmly she said: *'Main jaandi haan, samajh rahi haan, changa pehlan raj ke ro lai, pher baith ke galan karan ge.'*(I understand, I understand. Well, well, first you cry yourself out fully; then we shall talk at length.) And she hung up.

I could not tell her what was going through my mind. If my poems touched the heart of a person whose name is

'Amrita Pritam' I was honoured. I felt highly privileged. The poems she talked about were from the manuscript of my book *The Mindscape*. This is a coffee-table book of poems and paintings. A presentation of twenty-seven love poems and twenty-seven paintings. It is an effort to translate the mood of the paintings into poems and vice versa—a duet of words and images. In a way it was a quiet endeavour to evoke some kind of silent energy.

During one of my visits, I had left the manuscript on Amrita's table. I was hoping that when she felt better or when she felt inclined she would read the poems and perhaps comment. When I went to meet her that afternoon she gave me a paper which carried the following lines: 'From the "rim of vastness", "drop by drop", you who could "breathe the silence" must have experienced God as fragrance of love and for that I love you, Uma—Amrita Pritam.'

'Breathe the silence' she had picked up from my poem 'Silence', where I had written:

It floats over me
Engulfs me
Through the stillness
I walk towards you
Then held tight
I breathe the perfect silence

Amrita picked up the manuscript and said, 'I want to know from you about your poem 'High Point'. Softly she started reading the poem from the manuscript:

From the rim of vastness drop by drop
I fall towards you
In you
You become I
I you
Ever changing
Waves that touch and part
To meet again
And again

She finished reading. After a few moments of silence, she said, 'Uma, have you spoken of your lost love or an eternal love, whom you meet again and again, and part to meet again?'

Now she was probing. My expression said, 'I don't know,' but my voice said, 'Perhaps both—in the sense when one is searching constantly.'

That evening when I left her house, I was searching my inner self restlessly.

Nine

On another day, I had another early morning telephone call. Even before I picked up the phone I had a feeling it must be from Amrita. It was her. As I picked up the phone, I heard Amrita's anxious voice. She said: 'Uma, Imroz's fever is not coming down. Doctor says his blood has to be tested. It is Sunday today and no pathological lab is open. What do I do?'

I told her that I would come to her as soon as possible and arrange to take the blood sample to a seven-day pathological lab. I requested her not to feel so anxious. Within the next few minutes she made three frantic calls to me. Imroz had viral fever. His fever had been continuous for a few days. Amrita herself was not well and was unable to walk without help. She could only call doctors and pathologists over the phone. She was extremely worried about Imroz's health.

Before driving to her house, I had called up a nearby pathological lab, and asked them to send a technician to her house and have a blood sample collected. When I reached her house, the technician was already there. Imroz looked

weak but cheerful. Amrita seemed worried but less anxious. With the help of test reports the doctor was able to prescribe appropriate medicines. Imroz started feeling better.

After two days when I went to meet them, Imroz was moving about—warm, cheerful and hospitable as usual. I requested him not to exert himself too much and take rest, as there is always a chance of relapse. I mentioned that he had to remain well for himself and Amrita. I let him know that Amrita became very anxious when he was not well. He laughed—his usual unpretentious, unaffected and hearty laughter.

As we were having tea, Imroz said with a gleam in his

eyes, 'I agree, I have to remain well for myself as well as for Majaa. She gets very anxious when I am sick. *Eh meri maa vee hai te dhee vee* (She is my mother as well as my daughter.)' After a pause he continued, 'She does not like anybody else to come close to her to nurse her.'

Amrita's physical strength was steadily decreasing every day and so was her emotional dependence increasing on Imroz. The two made a very touching impression. Amrita and Imroz: sitting together, serving each other, eating together, Imroz nursing her. Sometimes talking, sometimes silent, sometimes thoughtful with a distant look.

I have seen them in many moods. I also visualized and experienced bits and parts of Amrita's own soul through the characters in her stories and novels. I have noticed how over and over again Amrita herself becomes Sunderan of *Yatri*.

One observes that Amrita herself is the mother and the daughter of the hero of *Ik Savaal*. She is the hero's mother through her marriage to his father. When the father dies, she is given in marriage to the man of her own choice by the hero. She then becomes his daughter.

In another story, the lovelorn Rajshree becomes Hakkoo—Amrita'a dead aunt. And Hakkoo becomes Amrita herself, to whom Hakkoo unconsciously passes on the death wish.

Her own experience hidden in the experience of the hero of *Ak da Boota,* explains how human souls can be extended and expanded. Just as sometimes I myself become Amrita. I often cry with her pain and feel helpless because of her sickness. The memory of the lost sister of the hero, in *Ak da Boota*, becomes the old man's quilt, to cover his body in the shivering winter and reveals that nature binds us all with one thread.

Imroz and Amrita are bound by the same thread. A thread that has neither been soiled nor become frayed. Forty years have passed and they are still in love—a love relationship that did not require any consent of society. At times I experience a forceful communication between Imroz's silent but vibrant paintings, and the different characters carved by Amrita in her poems, stories and novels.

Each of my visits to Amrita's house and my interactions with her and Imroz gave me living glimpses of Amrita's writings. Giving new meaning to the songs she had written and the songs I had sung, and the characters she had created and the characters I had known.

Ten

During one of my visits to Amrita, I asked Imroz how he felt about Amrita's affection for Sahir and later for Sajjad. He just laughed over my question. 'I will tell you something—once Amrita told me that if she had got Sahir, she would not have got me. You know what I said? I certainly would have got you even if I had to pull you out from Sahir's house.'

He added, 'When you love someone and you are sure of your love, you do not count the obstacles on the way.' Softly, with a long thoughtful pause, in his own unique way, he continued, 'You know, Amrita gave her book to me to give to Sahir, when I went to Bombay. I very gladly took it and gave it to him.' After another thoughtful pause, he said, 'I knew how much Amrita cared for Sahir but I also knew how much I cared for Amrita.'

I asked him another question, 'You know, Amrita got inspiration from Sahir; she wrote, *'Sunehre'*, the book that brought her the Sahitya Akademi Award for Sahir. Also she openly talked about it. How did you fit into her life?'

He replied with a lost-in-thought look on his face, 'With Sahir her life was illusive but with me her life is real. He left her restless but with me she is fulfilled.'

I interrupted, 'Sahir is quite vividly featured in *Ik si Anita*, *Dilli Diyaan Galiyaan* and *Akhari Khat;* so is Sajjad Haider in *Neighbouring Beauty* and *Seven Years*.'

He continued, 'Sajjad also was a very close friend of Amrita since her radio days. A friend in the real sense. For the first time in Sajjad Haider's company Amrita realized that a poem does not only get created out of passion of love, it can come out of a deep friendship also.' After a short pause, he remarked, 'For him she had said, "Buy me a pair of wings, stranger, or come and live with me."'

After another thoughtful pause, he went on, 'He really cared for Amrita in a very special way. After partition, Sajjad wrote to Amrita from Pakistan, off and on, I know that. I know Sajjad braved the riots of 1947 to see Amrita. He wrote to her: *Mein ek urte hue pal ki mulakat ke liye tarsa hoon.* (I have been thirsting for a moment's meeting with you.) I know they could share their very personal problems with each other. I believe Amrita told him about me also. That is why when we wrote a joint letter to him he wrote back to me saying, "I have not had the pleasure of knowing you, my friend, but I know you from a composite picture Ami's (he used to call Amrita—Ami) letters have made. *Tera raqib tujhe saalam karte hai* (your rival salutes you)." Before his death, Haider returned Amrita's letters through a friend who was visiting India. When Haider's friend brought the letters to Amrita she handed them over to me to read. How could I have read them? I burnt them all.'

Taking a deep sip from his cup of tea, he continued: 'When Guru Dutt offered me a job in Bombay, I came to break the news to her. Amrita was silent for a while and then she told me a story. It was a story of two friends, one very handsome and the other not so. A beautiful girl gets attracted towards the handsome one, who takes help to win her over from his less good-looking friend who also loves her ardently, but does not express his love because of his looks. The girl is smitten by the handsome man and eventually marries him. But soon war breaks out and both the friends are sent to the front on duty. The husband regularly writes to his wife but all the letters are composed and written by the friend. Soon after, the husband dies in the battlefield. His gravely injured friend is brought to the hospital, where the girl goes to meet him. While remembering her dead husband, she shows all his letters to the friend. The friend starts reading them, it becomes dark soon but he still continues to read them because he knows the words by heart as they were all penned by him and not by the dead husband. Soon the friend's condition starts deteriorating, and he passes away. The girl says, "I loved only one man. But lost him twice."'

Sighing deeply, Imroz continued: 'She thought I did not understand the implication of the story, but I did. To me she only said, *"Sahir Bombay chala gaya, hoon toon vee ja reha hain!"* (Sahir went to Bombay and now you are also going!) There was a deep disappointment in her voice, which conveyed the feeling that those who go like this never return.'

After a long thoughtful pause he went on, 'I went to Bombay but I wrote to her on the third day that I was returning. I knew that if I did not return, I would lose Amrita.

She has never expressed her love openly to me and neither have I mine, to her. She wrote of it only in poems:

Winds in my city
You set my heart on fire
Why?
Have you come past his city?
Your every breath
Sings restlessness,
Why?
Have you come past the path
Love takes?

That was his side of the story. Later I came to know that every evening on the terrace of his house, Imroz would wait just to have a glimpse of the vehicle that brought Amrita from her office at the All India Radio. He would continue to stand and stare even after the vehicle went by. Here he waited for her and there she wrote for him:

Cuckoo my heart sings
My tongue suffers blisters forbidden
With pain I get ensnared.

For me each visit to Amrita's house was a journey to a new world of relationships.

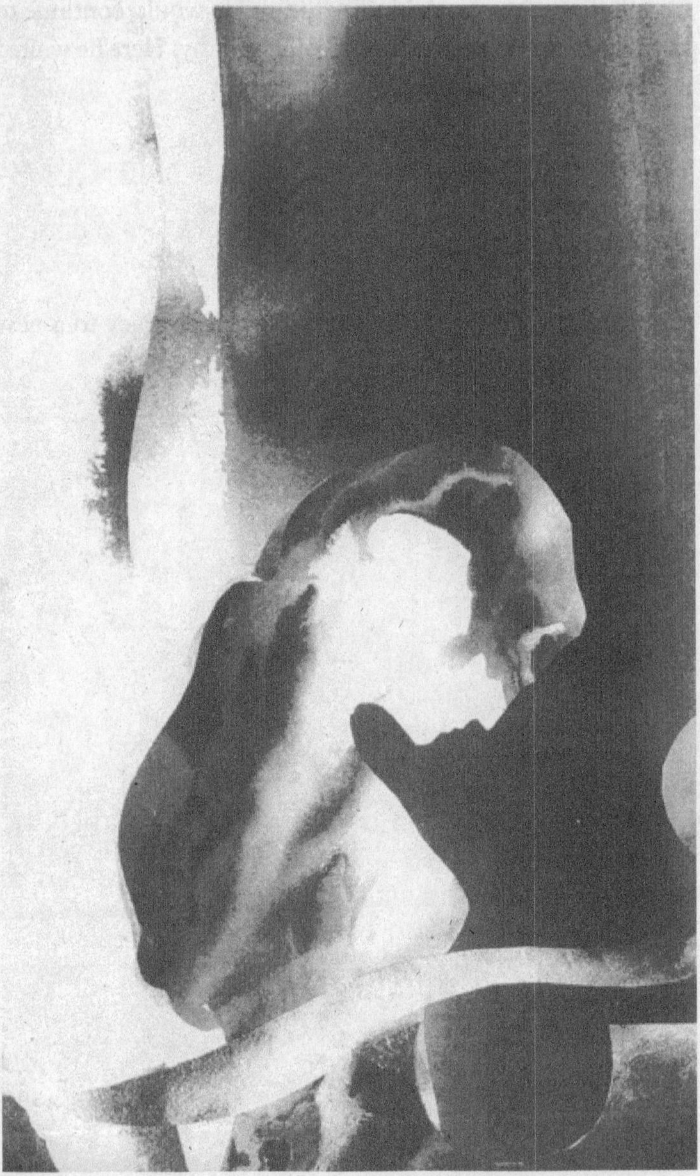

Eleven

One day when I went to Amrita, I found her quite weary and quiet. She was now confined to bed. She was not being able to move her legs on her own and even to turn on the bed she needed help. For her sitting up in bed was also difficult. But she liked to eat only while sitting. It was teatime and her daughter-in-law brought tea for her. Amrita these days took tea in a bowl with her favourite Nice biscuits.

I was admiring the red, flowery bowl, which she said she brought from Romania.

On and off her gaze became fixed on the hibiscus flower that peeped in from the window of her bedroom. After she finished the tea, I stroked her hand and helped her straighten her thin shrunken body. Looking at the flower, she softly said, '*Uma, teri patiyan wali nazam chete aa gai, jhehri Aishia Sultan ne gayee see. Zara ku, suna.*' (Uma, I am reminded of your poem on leaves, which has been sung by Aishia Sultan. Sing it, a little, for me.)

I hummed and then softly sang my poem 'Patte mere ghar aaye:

Patte mere ghar aaye
Chandani mein dhule
Geet bunte, jhanjhanate
Gungunate
Patte mere ghar aaye
Patte yoon hee bane rahe perh par
Phir bhi, jhankte, langhate
Khirki kee dehri paar kar
Samne kee diwar par
Dheeme sahme se dolte
Patte mere ghar aaye

She held my hand warmly as I was singing my poem. She was silent as I ended the first stanza.

She closed her eyes as I went on to the second and the third. As I finished, she slowly opened her eyes and said: 'Uma, how could you feel the pain, the parting, the friendship and the love of the leaves?'

I just looked at her in gratitude for the lovely words she had spoken and pressed her hands tenderly. Our eyes met and we communicated without words. She closed her eyes again.

She seemed lost in some far-off thoughts. Perhaps the poem reminded her of days gone by.

She lay there with her closed eyes for a while. I began with the healing and after about twenty minutes she desired to sit up again. Perhaps a little pent-up energy made her feel active. She had covered her head with a printed dupatta which served as a scarf. I had, in fact, suggested to her that she should wear reds and oranges so that her energy levels remained pepped up.

We discussed some current topics—her concern over pollution and the environment. We talked about the story and some characters of *Pinjar*—a film based on her story. After some time, she sat up, gave me a smile and asked me to recite something. I asked her what she would like to hear and she told me to choose whatever I felt like. I sang a few lines of a ghazal.

'What a sad verse!' she said. After a short silence she continued: 'I remember a very peculiar sadness on the face of a priest in Romania. Imroz and I visited a church there. The priest was hardly in his early twenties. He was so sad that I had to ask him why he was so. Imroz and I were returning from a function where I was presented a bottle of wine. We were carrying it and I offered some wine to the priest. We had no glasses but he accepted and drank it from the cupped palm of his hand. His face was completely plunged in despair. I did not want him to spread his depression all around and coaxed him into talking to me. He told me the story of how he became a priest.

'His heart lay somewhere else. Even religion did not soothe him. I told him to quit priesthood and leave as soon as possible. How could he have lived as a priest in that state of mind? I told him unhappiness was not his natural self, happiness was.'

Compelled life becomes compelling. In the story of the priest I found there was Amrita herself, who broke away from her life, which she did not like to live. Amrita, if she had wanted, could have continued to live in distress with her husband all her life but she made a bold choice, which required clarity of vision and, above all, courage. She must have known that as a public figure, she would have to face a lot of social criticism, anger and stigma.

One can get some glimpses of her anguish from poems such as *Breadwinner* and *Waiting*. These poems, perhaps, give us glimpses of her relationship with her husband. She writes:

Night half gone
Half to go;
I sit under the roof
Of your father and your father's father.
By dim candle light
Expecting your unsteady feet
The hateful smell of wine.
On your breath . . .
I, yes, I
I, the mother of your child to be born.

Amrita had once said, 'In which direction our life takes us, what side roads we turn into, knowing or not knowing whether they would be better or worse, depend on what choices we make at every stage of our life. And, if by chance, we make a wrong choice, we do not accept very easily that we made a wrong choice. On the contrary we often bring in factors to justify our mistakes, and if we do so, where shall we go?'

During all our interactions, Amrita never complained about her marriage. Not even to others, as far as I know. I

came to know much later that initially Amrita's husband did not agree to give her a divorce. It was much later, when he wanted to resettle with someone else that he agreed to do so.

Amrita did not have any grudge against her husband, it seemed. During the last stages of his life, when he was sick and alone, Amrita's son asked her if he could bring his father home to look after him. She not only agreed, but also herself nursed and supported him during his last days.

He breathed his last in her house.

In the same context, on another occasion, when I asked Imroz, he said, 'Why talk about someone whose life is of no concern to us, and our life of no concern to him or her?'

He was amazed at people who remained entangled with the lives of those who make them unhappy. Why do we let ourselves be affected by their lives and the unhappy situations they create for us? Why don't we resist those situations—actual or imaginary? We, in fact, live and relive those moments by relating them to others. As long as it is a catharsis, it is understandable but when it becomes repetitive, it becomes too much a part of our life. In fact it is like meditating on hatred.

Twelve

During various meetings with Amrita and Imroz, I came to know that Imroz was only nine years old when his mother died. Bereft of his mother's love he was left lonely and abandoned. His eyes searched for motherly affection everywhere. During his early schooldays, one of Imroz's class-fellows shared his paratha with him. He used to frequently enquire from his class-fellow as to who made the paratha for him. Every time his friend told him that his mother made the paratha, Imroz felt the presence and the emotional touch of his own mother.

Perhaps similar feelings got reflected many years later when Imroz accompanied Amrita after her work from All India Radio. That evening the staff car was late and Imroz suggested that they walk home in the moonlit night. Oblivious of others on the road and the heavy traffic, they both walked home from Parliament Street (Sansad Marg) to Patel Nagar, looking sometimes at each other, and sometimes at the full moon.

On reaching Amrita's house she shyly invited him to share her meal. Everybody else in the house, except the young

servant, had gone off to sleep leaving her meal on the table. The servant served whatever there was but there were only two chapattis. In a separate plate Amrita served one chapatti to Imroz but while eating the other she quietly served another half to him from her own. Imroz recollects the incident with great relish and says, 'Only the chapatti was half but the moon was full.'

On another occasion, when I asked Imroz what he liked

most about Amrita, he said, 'Her presence.' After a small pause, Imroz went on, 'When I was working for the magazine *Shama,* Amrita used to visit me sometimes in my office. She would look at me and then look at the paintings of women made by me, hung on the walls of my office, and my drawings published in the magazine. One day she put a question to me: "You paint women—beautiful women, with chiselled features; have you ever painted a woman with a mind?" I was taken aback. I had no answer to that question.

'After a while Amrita left. The question remained with me. Searching for the answer, I moved backwards into the past centuries of art. Glancing through the paintings of those times, which I had seen in the libraries of art schools and at the various museums, I could recollect only paintings of women, such as—woman with a sunflower, woman with a moon, woman with a child, woman with a smile. But, I did not find a woman with a mind. I was amazed that, for centuries, artists saw woman only as a body, and never as a mind.'

After a short silence, in a reminiscing mood, he created a vivid, romantic picture for me of an evening in the month of May in 1958 when the moon was full and the yellow flowers of *amaltas* (laburnum) hung on the trees, some on the earth and some blowing all around in the air. With a shimmer in his eyes Imroz said, 'Like the earth and the air, even Amrita looked so different. Everything was the same but the colours were brighter.'

They both walked and walked but they did not have to go anywhere. They spread themselves over the flowers on the earth and looked at the sky, sometimes with their eyes open and sometimes with them closed.

Creating another collage of memories he recalled: 'Alighting and ascending the stairs of the old monuments . . . from the terrace of such a building I watched the flowing Yamuna . . . she asked, "Have you ever come here with anyone else?"

'I replied: "To me it appears that I have never visited anywhere with anyone else—ever."

'We stopped and had tea . . . wherever we liked . . . every place seemed pretty . . . but beauty lay in the eyes of the beholder.'

Three days later, Imroz left for Bombay to work with producer-director Guru Dutt but quickly returned. As if returning to himself. Amrita was amazed and overjoyed. She looked at him, and continued to look at him for a long time, but never spoke a word.

Another collage of memories emerged: When it became inconvenient to carry Amrita's children to school on a two wheeler, because of the frequent *challan*s (fines) he had to pay on account of overloading, both he and Amrita decided to buy a car. They pooled in five thousand rupees each to buy a Fiat car for ten thousand rupees. The vehicle had to be registered in both their names. The registration officer asked him what his relation with Amrita was. When he replied that she was a friend the officer would not accept his explanation—how could friendship be a relationship between a man and a woman? It was a great dilemma for him.

I thought how strange it was that society cannot accept friendship as a relationship between two people.

Continuing with his memories of the same incident Imroz

recalled that he had filled a form for his insurance. In the column for a nominee, he had written Amrita's name, and in the column for relationship with the nominee, he had written the word 'friend'. The clerk objected. He wanted him to correct it by putting a relative's name. The objection came because it is not customary for a 'friend' to be a beneficiary in such a case. Imroz is not used to doing customary things anyway—that is why, for him, 'the bullfight', as he likes to term it, continued.

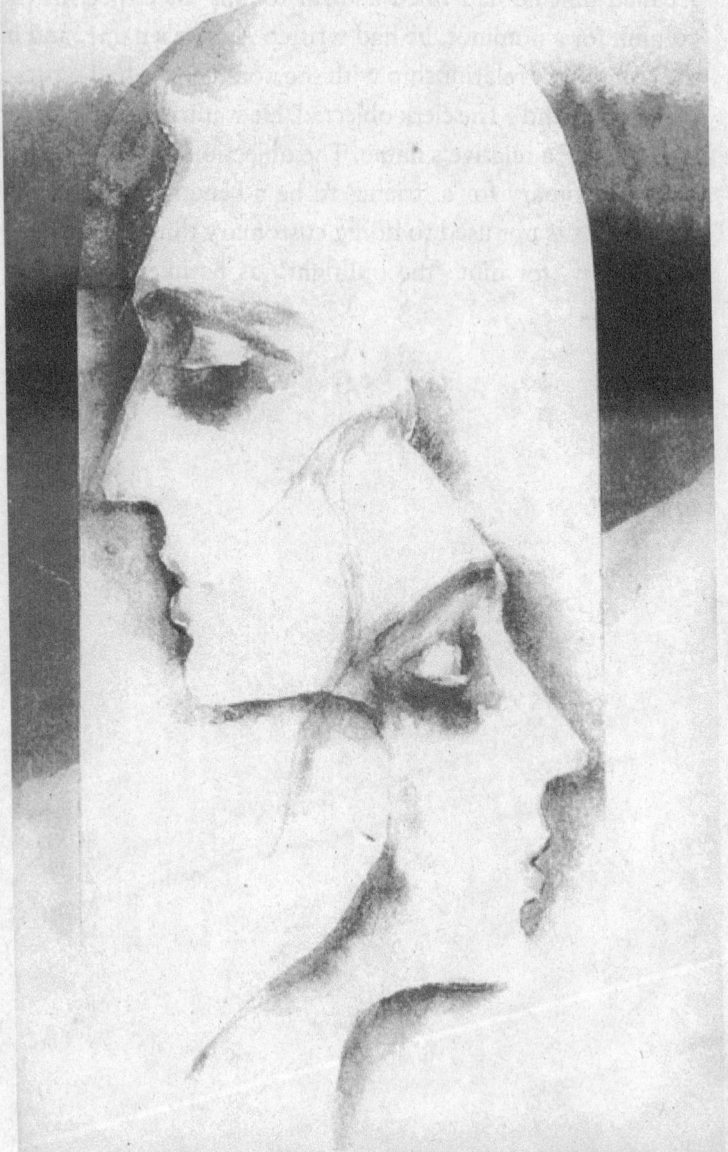

Thirteen

Imroz calls Amrita by many names. One of them is *Barkate,* which means 'good fortune' or abundance. 'Good fortune, she has in her hand, in her writing and above all in her being,' he says. He elaborates: 'The lines of Amrita's hardworking hands and the lines of her heart, her joys and sorrows, her desire to know, her prosperity, her accomplishment, all seem to cascade from the abundance of Gangotri, from where the river Ganga emerges.'

He goes on : 'Amrita is Heer as well as a fakir. (Amrita is the Heer of the love-legend *Heer-Ranjha,* as also a mendicant, a dervish.) *Takhat Hazaare*—the abode of the lover—is her religion and love is a way of life with her. By caste she is a mendicant and by temperament an amir. Whatever she earns with one hand, she distributes with two.'

Amrita and Imroz are similar and yet quite different in taste and temperament. They live in different rooms. Amrita works in the early hours of the morning when Imroz sleeps and Imroz works when it is time for Amrita to sleep. Their life rhythms are different. But they are also similar in many

ways: they both don't like to socialize and they don't like to go to parties, but nor are they alone, aloof people who like to spend time only in their own company. If a friend walks in when they are eating, he is most welcome to join them. But they don't observe any formalities, with each other or with anybody else. They both spend their time at home in their own rooms—she, in hers, writing, and he, in his, painting. The doors remain open. There is the fragrance of each other's presence but there is no interference.

When Amrita is working Imroz respects her privacy and

looks after the household chores. She writes sitting on her bed; so sometimes he quietly leaves a cup of hot tea by her bedside. For Amrita the creative writing can wait if her children need her attention. She will put a poem or story on hold to make a meal for the children, feed them properly and then return to her waiting poem. I remember she once said, 'All endeavour is creative—small things like cooking, mopping, sweeping are all creative—provided your attitude is creative.' For Amrita poems come on their own, she simply puts them on paper. She does not labour over them or craft them. She does not even revise them.

Imroz collects timepieces and changes their dials. In some clocks there are no numbers, instead there are couplets with pictures, and in others the numbers are tucked away in a corner to give space to the artist to write a couplet or a line.

Amrita collects statues like those of Lord Krishna in glass, Lord Ganesh carved in stone, Lord Buddha in sandalwood, and several small and big statues in various types of metals. She does not worship them, she just loves them. Imroz has made a big, beautiful painting of Lord Ganesh in which the Lord is playing the flute. Amrita is completely enamoured by this painting. It was published in one of Amrita's books. Seeing it in the book, some temple authorities had it enlarged and displayed in the various shrines of Lord Krishna in Lucknow. Amrita was thrilled and she remarked, 'Artists exhibit their work unnecessarily. A true exhibition is the one that people organize.'

She told Imroz, 'You wanted to be a folk song and there you are. . . . They do not know your name but your painting has reached the temples, on its own.'

Imroz's painting of Bahu's foot was carried to Lahore (Pakistan) by Shakeela. When the people from Bahu's tomb came to know of it they took it from her to adorn the walls of Bahu's shrine at Multan. Yet another friend from Lahore took Imroz's painting of Bulle Shah and now it beautifies the walls of Bulle Shah's shrine.

Is this why it is said that opposites attract each other? Is love then an attraction between two opposites?

Fourteen

A man has learnt only to sleep with a woman but has not awakened with her, was the answer given by Imroz to one of the readers of *Nagmani,* a magazine published by Amrita and Imroz. The question asked was—why is the man–woman relationship so entangled? For Imroz, a Punjabi with a rural upbringing, 'love is to get rooted, to grow, and blossom in the beloved's ground'. At another time, in another context, he had said: 'Most of us are not children born out of love. If we are born out of indifference, desire, anger, lust, jealousy or hatred, how can we love? To love we have to be born out of love.'

Amrita had always been escorted by Imroz wherever she went. If invited, Imroz would attend the function, otherwise he would wait for her outside, either in the lawn or in the parking lot. He would spend time reading a book of his choice. If it was a dinner engagement for Amrita, he would eat his packed meal either in the car or in the lawn. Doing this, he said, he never felt embarrassed or ill at ease. 'When you love,' he said, 'your ego dies, so it cannot come in between you and your beloved.' He elaborated: '*Prem gali saankari ja me do na samaye.*' (The love lane is narrow—two cannot pass through it.)

I had heard these lines many times before, but here they were being lived.

On another occasion Imroz had said: 'Ever since I met Amrita, the anger within me has disappeared. I don't know how. Perhaps the emotion of love is so strong that when you are filled with it, hatred, anger, jealousy all disappear. Just as there is no darkness when there is light around. When love brings happiness, peace and rejoicing, you don't talk harshly to anybody because there is no harshness within you.'

He went on, 'Do you know Rabia Basri? She was a famous saint who deleted a sentence from the Koran, which said "hate the devil". When asked why she did so, she replied, "I have no hatred in my heart and I see no devil," because, in her heart, only love prevailed.' He continued, 'By reading Buddhist scriptures we do not become Buddhas, and we do not become Krishnas by bowing before him. By bowing just for the sake of bowing, we become smaller. We have to invoke Buddhas and Krishnas within us. When they are awakened where will the devil be found?'

I went home that day with another perception, another view of love, as experienced by a lover.

Fifteen

Macmillan India had organized a function for the release of Amrita's autobiography in English. The publishers called me, specifically requesting me to persuade and somehow bring Amrita to the ceremony, but she refused, saying she was not well enough to go. When the publishers insisted I pleaded with her and tried to persuade her, but she held on to her decision. In the end, I emotionally cajoled her and ultimately she relented, on the condition that I pick her up and personally escort her to the function.

Trilok—my husband, whom she is very fond of—drove us all to the India Habitat Centre. Imroz and I escorted her to the venue of the ceremony—she was wearing a white salwar-kurta and could walk only very slowly. During the ceremony, Kapila Vatsayan requested her to recite her famous poem on the partition of 1947. I persuaded her to accept the request. Slowly Amrita started reciting her poem: *'Ik royee see dhee Punjab di'*.

The audience was spellbound and there was pin drop silence. With each word and each line Amrita seemed to be returning to her youthful vigour. Amrita's melodious and moving voice and the overflowing emotions of her poem, took us back to the agony of partition. It seemed that the apparently calm, docile Amrita still had a volatile volcano in her heart. She had the confidence to defy time and powerfully bring back the harsh realities of history.

People have put Amrita on a pedestal, they have denigrated her by writing fiercely against her, but they have never ignored her, nor have they left her alone. She was called *Awaaz-e-Punjab* (Voice of Punjab) and yet, this *Awaaz-e-Punjab* had to, ironically enough, leave Punjab. The objections were many, some real, some concocted.

Amrita is Sikh by birth and yet her hair is cut short; she smokes; she enjoys a drink once in a while; and, above all, she lives with a man who is younger than her, whom she loves, but is not married to.

Why did she have to suffer people's indignation? I fail to understand why people who had nothing to do with her life, gave her pain. While her books sold, and readers loved her, it seems her contemporaries could not digest her writings, the themes of her novels and stories, and her self-chosen style of life. There was hardly any newspaper or magazine in Punjab that did not make calumnious remarks on her lifestyle and her publications. Some of her writings were condemned and banned. There were many silent, as well as vocal, voices of protest against her 'sullied' name. But Imroz braved everything and stood by her. He held her hand through thick and thin and protected her from harm. In Imroz's presence she not only finds herself secure and safe but also emancipated.

About Imroz she writes: 'I will not attach "perfection" to you since it gives me the shuddering feeling of something cold and solid to which nothing can be added and from which nothing can be taken away . . . with you one can speak with ease . . . as if the very breath of my existence emanated from you. . . . As I sit writing to you from this foreign country it occurs to me that it is the fifteenth today, the day of our country's independence. Can one give a personality to this day? I would say you are 15th August for me since with you came the emancipation of the being . . . that is me. . . .'

Imroz knows Amrita needs support from him. So, like a large happy fountain of love, he showers himself on her and she, under his tender care, enjoys the cascade.

Imroz described a revealing incident to me: 'Once, we were travelling by car. Passing through Madhya Pradesh, when we reached the Maharashtra border, we were stopped by the police. Maharashtra at that time was a dry state. They wanted to check whether we were carrying liquor or any other intoxicant. After thoroughly checking they were fully satisfied that we did not possess any. But they did not know we were intoxicated by each other's presence. *Kee oh sada nasha utar sagde sun?'* (Could they have ever de-intoxicated us?)

Imroz described another incident when Amrita was watering the plants and, referring to her money plant, said, 'See how it grows like a creeper.' And he replied, 'You could make Waris Shah put out tendrils and shoots, this is after all a plant. . . .'

I wonder why society talks of change, yet it fears and rebels when change emerges? Amrita and Imroz represent a new social perspective. They speak a new and a different language of relationships—in thought and reality.

Sixteen

Saumya, my daughter, who had just finished her master's degree from the London School of Economics and Political Science (LSE), had returned home for a few weeks. She was soon to return for her PhD degree at the Manchester Business School. Her doctoral degree programme was being funded by the Cooperative Bank of United Kingdom. She had won the scholarship in a tough global competition.

I wanted to spend as much time with her as I could. But I also did not want to miss any of my healing days with Amrita. One afternoon both of us went to visit her. Amrita received Saumya very warmly and congratulated me for being the mother of such a smart and brilliant daughter. Amrita admires accomplishment.

She told Saumya to come close to her and then asked her to open the cupboard set against the wall of her bedroom. She asked her to bring out a bag from the cupboard. Opening the bag, she pulled out a velvet wallet from it. Giving it to Saumya she said: 'I had kept this for you, now you take it to

UK. It will be handy and useful.'

Saumya looked at me and then at Amrita. Accepting the wallet from her she placed it close to her chest and touching Amrita's feet in gratitude, asked for her blessings. Amrita held her hand lovingly and asked her to sit close to her. 'Sweet child,' she said. Saumya smiled. 'But does she listen to you?' she asked me jokingly.

'Sometimes she listens to me and sometimes I listen to her,' I said with a smile, and continued in the same tone, 'especially when she behaves like my mom, I listen to her.' We all laughed.

'Is she obstinate?' Amrita asked.

'Yes, in some ways, I let her be,' I said and then elaborated: 'In the sense, I do not stop her from doing what she wants to do. I only make her see the situation from my point of view also.'

'Saumya, what do you have to say?' Amrita asked.

'I think I am not obstinate but like to do things according to my point of view,' Saumya replied.

We all laughed again. After a few moments, embracing Saumya lovingly, Amrita asked me, 'She being the only child, why did you let her go so far from you?'

'I think I owe it to her. We wanted to give her an opportunity to soar as high as she likes or as high as she can, in the global environment. Also as she is the only child, and a girl, I want her to be a strong and independent person,' I replied.

In the meantime Amrita's daughter-in-law brought a soft drink for Saumya and all of us chatted on many different topics. After a while I asked the children to go to another room so that I could proceed with the healing session. Amrita felt better after the healing and called the children into the room. Putting her arms around Saumya, Amrita again asked her, 'Saumya, don't you feel homesick?'

'Yes, aunty, I do, but I believe I have to cope with it,' she replied.

'What have you thought regarding her marriage?' Amrita asked me.

'I feel we owe it to our daughters that they get an opportunity to find their own identity first and then identify their soul mates,' I replied.

Then, looking towards Saumya, she asked, 'What do you have to say about this, Saumya?'

Saumya smiled and said, 'I want to be able to walk on my own two feet first. Want to be professionally sound and economically independent.'

Continuing the same topic Amrita said, 'Perceptions and values are changing fast. Many new opportunities and professions have opened up for girls. I feel nowadays they have the opportunities to discover their full potential. This was missing during our time.'

Agreeing with Amrita I added, 'Yes I agree, and the fire in their hearts must be kept burning to search and express their own selves fully without fear or prejudice.'

Amrita smiled and said, 'Yes, I believe so. And the only way, I feel, is self-reliance through education. Otherwise how will they find unless they know what they are searching?' She further added, 'I have always said that a woman must be made independent and for that a woman must fight her battles on her own. If she wants independence, she must do something to get it, merely wanting is not enough.'

Elaborating on the subject of women's position in society, Amrita continued, 'I have always been against patriarchal domination, oppression and subjugation of women. In my own life I have always tried to earn my own livelihood. I am very critical of women for being economically dependent on men. If they are, they let themselves be used as men's playthings or be subjugated as their servants.'

I was happy to learn about Amrita's views on women's rights and her own values in life. More so as we had two young girls with us who seemed to agree with her point of view as well as mine. There did not seem to be any obvious generation gap. As Saumya drove me back, we found ourselves discussing the same topics, and agreeing on most.

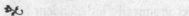

Seventeen

With time, I found I could discuss any topic freely and frankly with Amrita—even her personal and intimate life. I could imagine what happens to a mother when her children find her guilty of giving a new turn to her own life without bothering about their mental agony, which they undergo on account of that. When a home breaks, the tremors shake the psyche of the children. The personal and social adjustments which they have to make, for emotional tranquility and social acceptance, are enormous. Parents often forget the emotional and psychological limitations of their own children. It is normal for the children to accuse their parents of selfishness.

As a sensitive mother, Amrita suffered the suffering of her children. Hiding her own anguish, she consoled them, brought them up well, and provided them with all that was required single-handedly. She could not create a normal natural environment where a father and a mother were together to look after their children because the father of the children was not there and she had to play the role of a mother as well as that of a father. She had to explain to the children that a tortured, tormented and an unhappy mother could not have given them anything better than what she had herself. So, to give them love and affection, she needed to create some space for the same in her own life.

She was a doting mother. Money did not come easy and she had to earn it with great difficulty and with lot of hard work. Yet, when it came to spending it on her children, she was very generous. When her son graduated in architecture, he desired to go to Europe for a holiday. She immediately called up the travel agent and made all arrangements for his trip to Europe. She says, 'I have tried to provide my children as much happiness as I could search for or gather.'

Amrita's honesty and courage steered her through the difficult times. She had to pass through many rough and emotionally disturbing times while bringing up her children. When her son was born, she imagined him to be looking like Sahir. She believed that if she fixed Sahir's face in her mind's eye, he would grow up to resemble him. But one cannot live forever in an imagined world. When one day he asked her point blank whether he was Sahir's son, she said 'No'.

She told him the truth. With her emphatic truthful 'No' she wondered whether imaginative truth was in any way less powerful than truth itself. As far as possible, Amrita tried to save her children from the scandalous remarks of people. With Imroz providing the much-needed support to her in his own quiet, gracious manner, Amrita could bring up her children in a happy balanced way.

Imroz says, 'Amrita's children are mine too. So whatever I did, I did for our children.'

When asked 'Didn't you want your own children?' he laughs and says, 'We already had children when we met, so where was the need to have more?'

Once, in a contemplative mood, Imroz had said, 'At the wedding of Amrita's son, seeing the reluctance of the family members, I quietly withdrew myself from attending the marriage ceremony, knowing that their relations and society at large were not mature enough to accept the fact that I was a friend of Amrita.' He laughed and explained, 'Also, if I had gone with the marriage party, who would have decorated the newly wedded couple's room with flowers? So, it was good I stayed back.'

That day I left Amrita's house with mixed feelings and many unanswered questions. Deep in my heart, I could feel the agony of a mother, the anguish of a woman suffering for her children and the difficulty of Imroz's predicament.

Who was right? Was anyone wrong? As I drove home that day I was confused, to say the least.

Eighteen

The more I know Amrita, the more I love her. And the more confused I become. Because more questions come to my mind. She fascinates me.

Amrita once mentioned to Imroz that if something happened to her he should resettle with someone else. Imroz was silent for a while and then replied, 'Who, by the way, do you take me for? A Parsee . . . ? That I must be thrown to the vultures to be pecked at . . . ? You have no business to die on my hands like this . . . I must see the film through . . . you promise me that you are going to jog along until we are ready to go together.'

Amrita's health was slowly deteriorating. She was now so sick that she could neither walk nor sit on her own. It is Imroz who helps her take a turn in her bed. He feeds her with his own hands, bathes her, changes her clothes and nurses her. He does it all so lovingly that he has made it into a joy. For him, it is just like bringing up a little baby.

Amrita has a very tiny appetite—her intake of water and food is very little. When, for a number of days, she did not eat well, the doctor found her slightly dehydrated and suggested that she be hospitalized for a few days. She was admitted to a nearby nursing home but she did not like it there. On the third day she insisted that she be discharged and taken home. But on returning home, she was quite listless and weak. During this time, while giving her healing, I found that she was not responding positively to it. I was apprehensive.

On returning home I shared my anxiety with my reiki guru, Mrs Renoo Nirula. She, like Amrita, has been my source of inspiration. In spite of her busy schedule, she readily agreed to come with me to give healing to Amrita. Fortunately, Amrita responded well to her treatment. Renooji continued to visit her off and on. Both Imroz and I would try and comfort Amrita in our own different ways.

Imroz has never pronounced his love for Amrita and neither has she for him. Imroz had once told her: 'There can be no one else . . . *no* one. . . . You are my daughter . . . I . . . your son.' Yet people degraded their friendship. Amrita confesses: 'My suffering is the lesser truth when weighed against the greater truth . . . the happiness of my life with Imroz.' Why should they be expected to take society's permission to experience such happiness? Imroz believes that there is no room for society's consent or interference when one chooses a path for oneself. Hesitation insults the feet as well as the path.

Once somebody told Amrita that at the time when she was born, the moon was in the house of fate. She exclaimed, 'Then Imroz entered the house of fate and Imroz did not budge once he entered—the moon is of a different mould altogether, flitting from house to house.'

As their joke goes, Amrita and Imroz have enjoyed their lives as guests at God's wedding. Fully immersed in the fun and frolic of the wedding they are enjoying and rejoicing as if that was the very purpose of their lives—individually as well as together—each one giving the other enough time and space to grow. The only difference in their status is that she is attending the wedding from the groom's side and he from the bride's. That is why, perhaps, as part of the custom, it is Imroz who has to look after Amrita. Throughout their lives they have done things together like keeping the house, looking after the children, gardening and cooking.

He does the purchasing of the vegetables and she used to do the chopping, when she could—he the seasoning and she the stirring, he the lighting of the fire and she the baking. It was Imroz who inspired her to do their cooking together.

As I drove home that day I felt elated to be a small part of that little nest, and its little love story.

Nineteen

Conversations between Amrita and Imroz, as well as their observations of each other, fascinate me. Once Amrita said to Imroz, 'You are my only friend.'

Imroz in turn asked, 'How come you placed your faith in me?'

'Didn't you yourself say that you were Dr Dev of my novel of the same name? I had written the novel much before I met you. But out of a perfidious crowd, didn't I pick you? Isn't it proof enough?' replied Amrita.

In another setting, she picked a couplet by Faiz to recite:

Kisi ka dard ho karten hain tare naam rakam
Gila hai jo bhi kisi se, tere sabab se hai.

(No matter whose pain, it is on your account
No matter whose complaint, you are the cause)

So, for Amrita, Imroz becomes answerable to all the wrong that happens—whatever, wherever.

Be it the misconduct of a driver or a conductor of a bus (reported in the paper or shown on television) with a lone woman who repels them and throws herself out of the running bus or be it China's cunning, Russia's deception, America's despotism or Pakistan's lies—she gets angry with him.

On the other hand, Imroz says: 'She is a born idealist. Out of bitterness, she may say whatever she likes but no amount of breach of faith has shattered her inner belief in the goodness of people. Her exterior may burn like a flame of fire but inside she is calm and cool.'

He goes on to elaborate on his observations: 'When the time comes, she places her faith in life. In most cases though she consoles herself by writing an elegy.' In another context, Imroz had said: '. . . at the same time, the extent of affinity or kinship she has towards her own contemporaries is abounding. So much so that if she likes a poem or a couplet written by any of them, revelling in it, she would hum it out to everybody as if someone close to her heart has accomplished a great literary achievement. While admiring it so, she herself shines like the sunshine. Whereas, they [her contemporaries] are so very hard-hearted and narrow-minded towards her.'

According to Imroz 'Amrita never liked to live off anybody. Men do not understand the value of independence for women, particularly the women of the house. They accept their income very easily but never their independence.'

In Lahore, when she went to the radio station for programmes, an elderly member of her family called her one day and asked her how much she earned for a programme.

When she replied she earned ten rupees he told her to take twenty rupees from him and stop going to the radio station. But she did not agree because, for her, her independence and self-reliance mattered more than money.

A point on which both Amrita and Imroz concur is their belief that religion and parents as well as society condition children, so that they remain under control. But it is forgotten that no healthy relationship can be formed with scared children and a scared society. A relationship develops only when it is unaffected, natural and instinctive. Imroz believes that if one is scared of somebody, whether it is one's parents or God, one cannot love. With the conditioning of parents and the restrictions of religion, no man or woman is free. Imroz once said, 'Freedom, as most understand, is simply a piece of cloth. A colourful flag hoisted in so-called free countries.'

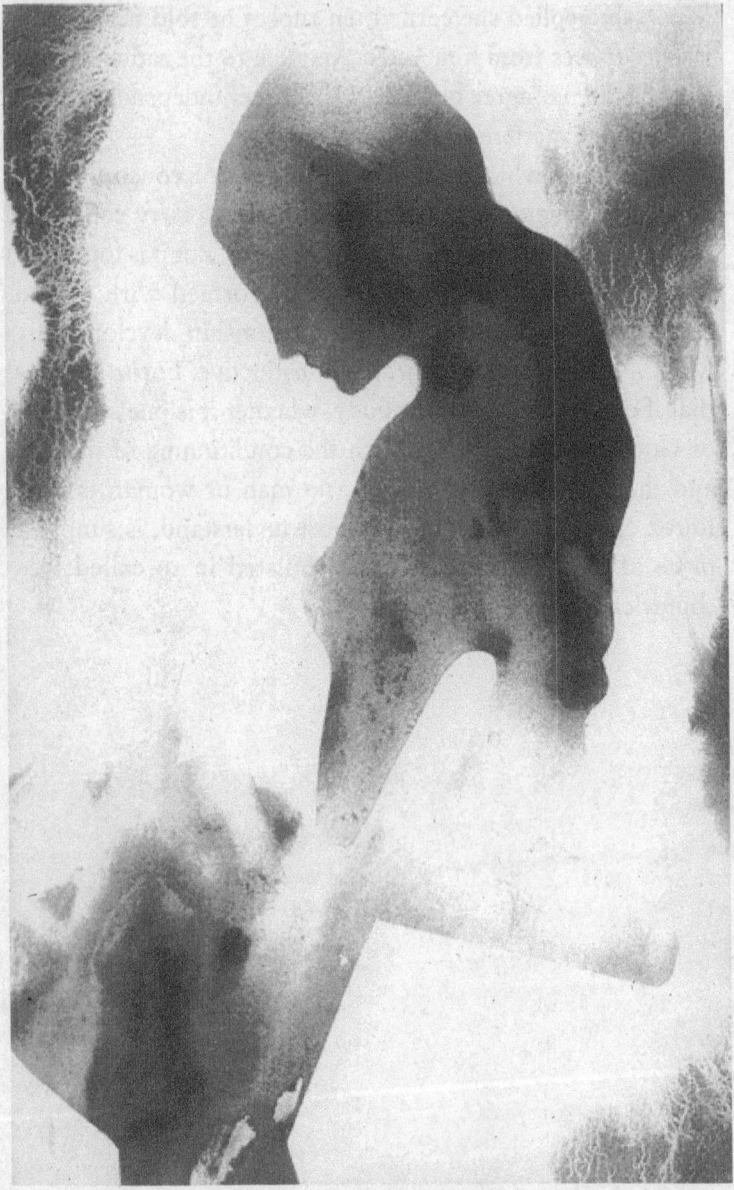

Twenty

Amrita grew up alone. Her mother died when she was ten years old—so she was denied a childhood. Her father was a writer who wrote at night and slept during the day. There were only books all around her in which she buried herself. She felt like a book herself, but a blank one. So she started writing on its pages.

Her father recognized her talent, nurtured it, taught her rhyme and the metre, goaded her to sing about God and of the agony of mankind. He wanted her to be Mirabai, which she could not be. She carved an image of 'a Rajan', an imaginary friend, whom she searched out from the shadows of the moon, and at which she gazed for endless nights.

She wrote her first one-line love poem for her Rajan at the age of eleven. When her father found it in the pocket of her shirt, she was scared and afraid to admit that she had written the poem. Her father slapped her—not for having written the poem, but for having told a lie. Amrita says, 'My poem could not bear the fact that I had lied, it emerged and began to reveal itself, unabashed.'

Amrita did not like restrictions. Her father who was a staunch Sikh, took her under his care to teach her the daily prayers. It was a ritual that was strictly observed, especially the evening prayers, which were taken more seriously because they were supposed to provide a shield all through the night to the person from all outside evils.

But Amrita's young mind did not want to be fully protected or shielded by the prayers because she wanted her Rajan to come into her dreams at night. So she would skip one or two lines of the prayer so that some space was left for Rajan through which to enter her dreams.

As an adult Amrita was a bold, outspoken person who

did not care a bit for what others said about her. Her style of life, her lack of discretion in emotional matters, her honesty and fearlessness, her short hair, the trousers she wore, her smoking and drinking were all responsible for the controversy that surrounded her persona throughout her life. She was vehemently criticized by men who could not appreciate a woman with a mind. She firmly believes that a man admires a beautiful woman, worships a distant goddess, and uses a wife as a slave.

Amrita is a proud Punjabi and she identifies herself with the people of Punjab. She is a child of the undivided Punjab. She talks of Punjab as the great land of the five rivers, where *Niti Shastra*, the first book of grammar, and the first book of the world, the *Rig Veda*, were written. Branded for her candid views on religion and fundamentalism and detested for her outrageous honesty, Amrita, a proud daughter of Punjab, was befittingly honoured as *Awaaz-e-Punjab* and once again given public appreciation after a long lapse of time.

The Punjab government awarded her with a lifetime achievement award, which was conferred on her by the chief minister of Punjab himself. He came personally to confer the award on her at her residence and Amrita was moved by this gesture by her native state. She was quite unwell that day and had to be brought to her drawing room on a wheelchair. The vice chancellor of Punjabi University, Patiala, and some other writers of Delhi and Punjab had come to witness the ceremony along with the chief minister.

At the ceremony Amrita made a moving remark: '*Bahut salan baad mere paikiaan ne mainu yaad keeta hai, par ainee der kar ditti ke hun mein khari ho ke tuhaada istekbal vee nahin kar sakdi.'* (After a long time my paternal state remembered me. But it is delayed so much that I am now not even able to stand up on my feet to welcome you.)

As I drove back that day, I felt especially proud of being a Punjabi, as also to have witnessed and emotionally experienced a small part of its long literary history.

Twenty-one

I saw Sahir's name beautifully calligraphed and displayed in Imroz's room. As I was looking at it, Imroz noticed a surprised look on my face and also a question mark. He understood what I wanted to ask!

'You must be wondering why I have calligraphed Sahir's name,' he said. 'You know,' he went on, 'when Amrita is not writing on a paper, the forefinger of her right hand automatically writes a word, a name—anybody's name, or even her own. Again and again her finger writes on everything, reachable or unreachable, whatever comes in front, ranging from her knee to my shoulder, from the walls of her room to the walls everywhere, from this generation to the other generation. So much so that her finger reaches out to the plants, the leaves, the fragrance; she seems to be writing on everything.'

She herself had told me that the shadows in the moon appeared like words to her. In her childhood, her index finger made words out of those shadows. What sort of a composition was this? What sort of worship?

Imroz continued, 'During our earlier days, I used to transport her on my two-wheeler. While sitting at the back one day, her index finger wrote 'Sahir' on my back. I immediately realized how much she loved him. So, whosoever is loved by Amrita has a place in our house, in our hearts.'

Imroz designed the jacket of Sahir's book *Aao Koyee Khwaab Buneih* (Come, Let's Weave a Dream). Knowing Amrita's feelings for him, Imroz smilingly remarked: 'Why weave a dream when one cannot be the dream of someone.'

Amrita's relationship with Sahir was one of silence. It was essentially on a mental level. There was nothing physical in their bond. For her he had a God-like image. He was the tall man in whose long shadow she walked and found joy and sustenance.

For fourteen years she walked in this shadow. There was a silent communication between the two. He would come, give his poems and go. At times, he would walk up to a paan shop on her street; have a soda, a paan or a cigarette, gaze at her window and return. He was an integral part of her. Yet, he remained, for her, a star—constant, visible but distant.

As Amrita herself has mentioned Sahir would come to her house, sit in a chair, smoke cigarette after cigarette and leave the butts in the ashtray and go. After he left, she would pick them up one by one and smoke them. That is how, she says, she got into the habit of smoking.

Amrita believed in strong individuality in love. Discussing love one day she said, 'No one merges. The two individuals are separate. Only by being separate, can they recognize and love each other. If you merge, whom do you love?'

Amrita's image of a lover is very strong and passionate. She writes:

Chadar phateyan mein takiyan laawan
Ambar phate kya seena?
Khavind mare hor karan mein
Ashiq mare kina jeena?

(I can patch a sheet if torn
But can I stitch the sky?
A husband dies, I remarry
A lover dies, can I live?)

One day, I asked Imroz, 'Amrita lived with the memory of Sahir, did it bother you?'

'No. I accepted it. There is no hassle when one loves without ego, without argument, without making artificial arrangements, and without calculations,' he replied. 'There is no problem when one lives in *sehaj bhav*.'

I could not understand what he meant by *sehaj bhav*. When I asked him, he explained it to me with a story:

'There was a fakir, who came to live in a village. He sat under a tree and meditated. The villagers provided him with whatever they could afford. During this time a landlord's young daughter fell in love with someone. Without getting married to her lover she gave birth to his illegitimate child. The family was shamed. The whole village raged at her. They wanted to know the name of the man who had played with her honour. Out of fear, the girl did not disclose the name of her lover. Her family was furious. When they kept insisting, out of desperation she took the name of the fakir. When the villagers heard this they got really mad at him and beat him up severely and handed over the illegitimate child to him. The fakir did not say anything in his defence. He did not object. He accepted the child as his own and took him in his arms. The fakir had no means and depended upon the villagers for sustenance by begging from door to door. But now, the villagers were very harsh towards him. Wherever he went he found doors closed on his face. One day when he passed by the door of the landlord, the mother of the child heard the cries of the baby. She became very restless and came running to feed her hungry baby. While doing this, she cried and admitted that her child was not from the fakir but from her own lover. The villagers felt repentant and asked for forgiveness from the fakir.'

After a pause, Imroz said, 'See, the fakir accepted the child, accepted the blame and carried on. That is being *sehaj*,' Imroz went on to explain, '*Jis ko koyee faraq hee naa pare, vahee sehaj ho sakta hai.*' (He who accepts unquestioningly lives in *sehaj bhav*.) I thought how difficult it is to accept—but perhaps it is this acceptance, which raises the spiritual status of a human being.

On another occasion, I asked Imroz, 'Amritaji received so much admiration from all over, didn't you also want similar societal appreciation?'

'Do you know Uma, Osho was never televised or invited to address gatherings, never was he honoured or awarded by any organization or government. Yet, he has been continuously read and heard by millions of people around the world. His words have been translated into almost all major languages of the world.' He continued after a short pause, 'How does one explain society's approval or disapproval? Does it have any consequence?'

He then went on to explain his stance with a poem:

Mein ik lok geet,
Be-nau, hawa vich khara
Hawa da hissa
Jeenu changa lagan
Oh chete bana lave
Hor changa lagan
Te apnaa vee lave
Jee awae tan gaa vee lave
Mein ik lok geet.
Siraf lok geet.

Jeenu nau dee
Kadi lor nahi paindee.

(I am an unnamed folk song,
A part of the flowing breeze,
Those who appreciate me
May remember me,
Those who admire me
May own me
Those who cherish me
May even sing me
I am a folk song
Just a folk song
That does not require any name.)

Love . . . how many varieties and dimensions does it have? As I drove back from their home that day this question echoed in my mind.

Twenty-two

At a literary meet I overheard a writer comment on Imroz as a 'kept man'.

To me it seemed as if somebody had rudely crushed a delicate and a beautiful object. My endurance shrieked in protest. Emotionally disturbed, I wondered—what is a 'kept' man or woman? The one who is economically dependent? Socially weak? Intellectually inferior whom the other partner can subjugate? Or the one whom the other can dominate—sexually or otherwise? There did not seem to be any such element in Amrita and Imroz's relationship.

In the 1950s when Imroz and Amrita met, he was earning almost twelve times more than Amrita. Imroz had no family responsibility to fulfil, whereas Amrita was married and had two children.

Amrita had yet to establish herself as a writer. On the other hand, at that time Imroz was an acclaimed painter and was professionally in demand. Intelligent, well informed and good-looking, he had an identity of his own. So I wondered—how could he be a kept man?

During the more than forty years of their life together, Imroz did not spend even a penny from Amrita's earnings on his own personal needs. During my various conversations with Amrita, she had related an instance to me. Once, when Imroz did not receive his payments in time, and did not have enough money to purchase things for the household, she had quietly placed some money in his pocket and told him that he could return the same when his payments arrived. She vividly recalled that Imroz did not even touch that money. On the contrary, when he returned, he came to her and told her to take the money out from his pocket herself because he had managed without it.

I wondered how people could label such a relationship as 'kept'. Why cannot a man and a woman be together as just friends?

I had once mentioned to Imroz, '*Log kehte hai ke aap ne sari zindagi Amrita ko pankha karte karte hi guzar dee.*' (People say that you have spent all your life fanning [cheering] Amrita.)

After a few moments of silence, he smiled and said, '*Woh nahi jante ki pankha karte karte hawa mujhe bhi to aayee.*' (They do not know that while fanning her, I also received the breeze.)

I felt deeply touched by the sentiments expressed by him. I felt it was a boon and a divine gift offered only to the very privileged. It is only in the temperament of a dervish to understand such a sentiment.

Twenty-three

One day when I went to Amrita's house, an air conditioner was being fitted in Imroz's room. To avoid the noise he had come to sit in Amrita's room and started narrating an incident: 'When I was studying at the art school in Lahore, I used to spend my summer vacation in my village, where I grazed cattle—not only my own but also my uncle's. I would leisurely continue to sketch and the cattle would graze on their own.'

Amrita laughed and said, 'Like Ranjha, you played the *vajhali* (musical instrument) and the cattle grazed on their own?'

Imroz also laughed and replied, 'Yes, but there was no Heer to feed me with *choori* (a sweet made out of chapatti, butter oil and sugar).'

'Were you not fond of any girl in the art school?' she asked.

'Some girls came to the school for short spans of time, in pursuit of their hobby, but they came seldom,' he replied.

He suddenly went into a lane of distant memories and

said, 'One of them was a girl named Manjit. I had glimpses of her from a distance, but never went close to her.' He paused again and continued, 'I came to know that she was the daughter of a rich man. So, there was no question of my talking to her. I could only look at her from a distance. But I prefixed the first letter of her name, M, to my name as M-Inderjeet.'

Amrita remarked, 'What an unfortunate girl! Didn't she know that an angel was gazing at her?'

'She didn't have your eyes,' he concluded.

How M-Inderjeet became Imroz is a long story. In school, there were three Inderjeets in his class. The teacher had to take the roll call as Inderjeet one, Inderjeet two, and Inderjeet three. It was inconvenient for them as well as for the teacher. He wondered why his name was Inderjeet? Perhaps, it was just a name that occurred to his parents.

Imroz is a Persian word which means 'today'. He liked the word because it did not have any connection with a character in mythology or history. It also did not spring out of a God's name—like a Ram Prasad, Krishan Chandra, or a Mohammad Ali.

The word Imroz does not have a past history or a future reference. It means the present, the 'now'. Imroz believes only in now. He does not believe in binding himself with the rigidity of past traditions or the remote future. He says he lives for today.

However, once, while calligraphing his own name, he divided the word into three parts:

Imr|O|Z

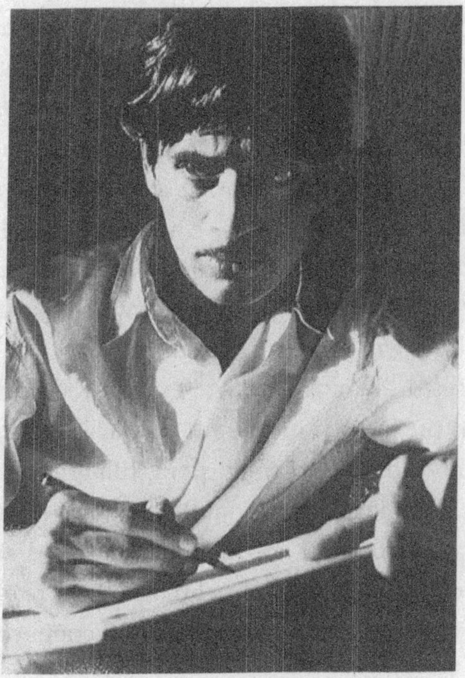

Imr suggests the past. O, the present, pulsating and alive. It is golden in colour and a little elevated from the rest of the alphabets. An indicator of the recognition of the self. Z has an empty space in front of it, as if a space for the unknown future.

Inderjeet became Imroz in 1966.

Whatever Imroz touches, he turns into a piece of art. Some time ago he made lampshades over which he painted lines of Faiz, Firaq, Amrita, Shiv Batalvi and other poets. One of the many lampshades that he has made is a square one with glass panels painted in red. On its four sides he has written one line each of four poets. The line from Waris Shah is: '*Jadon ishque de kam nu hath layiye pehle rub da na dehaiye ji.'* (When love calls for action, begin it with the name of God.) Shah Hussain's line is: *'Hanju roande har koyee ashik roande ratt.'* (Everyone sheds tears, lovers, drops of blood.) Shiv Batalvi's lines are: *'Aj din chhariya tere rang warga.'* (Today dawned as bright as you.) And Amrita's lines are: *'Parchhawayian nu pakran walio, chhatti ch baldi ag de parchaven nahin hunde.'* (Flames within the heart have no shadows, how will you catch them.)

Imroz filled the engraved words with red colour. When the bulb of the lamp is lit, the red colour is reflected on the glass windows of the drawing room, filling it up fully with red colour. One day Amrita impulsively went to Imroz's table where he was working, not minding his soiled and colour-smudged clothes. She stood behind him and touching his shoulders clung to him and asked: 'How come you met me, Imroz?'

In his own brief way he replied: 'Just as you met me.'

But then he continued, 'Do you know, Majaa, when I finished my course at the Lahore Art School all the students left for their respective homes at the end of the term, but I continued to occupy the hostel room. In fact I had not found a job and I did not want to return to the village. One evening, the warden came to my room and told me that I could not continue to stay in the hostel as the term was over. I did not know where to go at that time. Also, my heart did not permit me to stay there any more. I immediately walked towards the railway station and asked for a return ticket, to go to any nearby place, simply to pass the night on the train, so that I could make an alternative arrangement for my stay in the morning. Do you know, the booking clerk gave me a return ticket to Gujranwala—the place of your birth? Do you realize how destiny was trying to point me towards you?'

Looking at Imroz making a portrait of a woman Amrita once asked him: 'Have you become a captive of this theme?'

'No, I have not, I am going along with it,' he replied.

'Some artists do not like to make portraits of others, they think, in that case, they get married to the portrait,' Amrita commented:

'In my view, it is not marriage, it is love,' he replied.

'But love is also divine marriage,' she said.

'If you can use the word divine with marriage, you may call marriage, love,' was his reply.

'After traversing through the six charkas, yogis believe that when they reach the seventh, there is marriage of Shiv and Shakti,' she said.

'If the union of Shiv and Shakti can be called marriage, I do not mind,' he remarked.

It seems Imroz does not believe in the customary concept of marriage. For him love seems to be complete in itself. On another occasion, Amrita inquired, 'Some particular colour is very dear to some painters, and that becomes their favourite colour. Like some famous painter said, he liked red, so much so, that he wanted to paint everything red. Do you have any such preferences?'

'The colour of the sunshine surrounds me. I want to colour everything in it. Perhaps it is because I associate you with sunshine.'

They both laughed.

When Imroz is asked why he does not like to exhibit his paintings he laughs and says: 'You exhibit for two reasons, one, to know the opinion of others and second, to sell the paintings. I do not seek approval of others, and I do not paint to sell. Then why should I exhibit? Also, I do not like the word "exhibit."'

When asked how his paintings would reach the viewers he replies: 'Art does not seek viewers, viewers seek art.' When asked why artists have so many love affairs his reply is: 'The difficulty with artists is that they don't love anybody. They want to be loved by everybody, each time. I believe love means loving your loved one, unconditionally, once and always.'

Commenting on Imroz's love for painting nature Amrita says: 'I believe it is his memory of the Garden of Eden which is seeking expression in his colours. Beauty, which I see in his paintings, is perhaps the same he saw in the Garden of Eden.' She adds, 'Apple was known to be the forbidden fruit on account of which Adam and Eve were thrown out of the Garden of Eden. It seems, in his case, it was not the apple. It must have been the grapes.' Imroz has an inherent love for grapes.

In earlier days if somebody wanted to meet Imroz, he or she would phone Amrita and ask: 'Is it Amrita's house?'

She would say, 'Yes it is.'

Then the person would ask: 'Is Imrozji there?'

And she would say, 'Yes.'

Then she would cling to Imroz and say, 'See, people now find your house at my address.'

For me, a different kind of love story was being unfolded in bits and pieces. Perhaps a modern-day living legend of Heer–Ranjha or Sohni–Mahiwal.

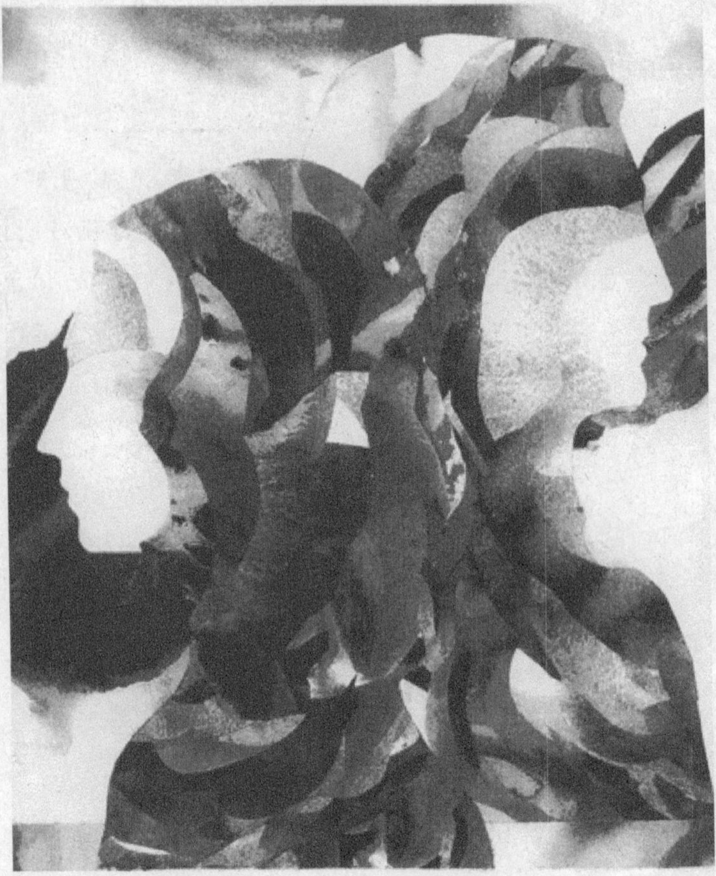

Twenty-four

It seems, love moved on its own. It did not take any directions from anywhere. No one planned it or guided it. Which way did Amrita move? With whom did she move? She did not know.

She did not know Imroz at that time; his thoughts or his frame of mind; his ways were unknown to her. One day when they were together she had asked him, 'When you were born in a farmer's house, why did you pick up paint and brush in place of the plough?'

Laughing he had replied: 'Even now I am doing the same, ploughing over the earth of thoughts, on the land of imagination. When I was small, there was nobody around. I would draw and paint for hours sitting alone. I could see only the fields and the ploughs.'

'Didn't you paint women?' she asked

'No. Only fields and ploughs. They alone were the objects of my attention at that time.'

One day, while painting, Imroz put a bindi on her forehead with his brush. She laughed. That day, her forehead became his canvas. Looking in the mirror, she had seen a bindi on her forehead for the first time. Something stirred in her mind and she put a question to him, 'How would you elucidate reality.'

'By seeing another reality out of one reality,' he replied.

Perhaps he was right. The reality of lines and colours is also a reality. As for her, there was reality in the sound of words. Every reality is born out of an existing reality, provided that the artist has the eye to see it. Just like a philosopher can see a tomorrow in today.

For some, the abstract is reality. Like Pablo Picasso, who hung the saddle of a tricycle in the middle of its handle. The shape of a bull's head was visible in the centre. He drew out the reality of a bull's head from the reality of a tricycle. This he called the journey of the imagination. When inner vision mingles with external objects, many shapes erupt. Though the words are few, thousands of imaginative phrases take shape from them.

When a poem or a story is written, it first moves and mingles in the mind and when its form and shape fit only into the reality of the imagination, is it put on paper.

Amrita had once asked Imroz, 'Before you submit your canvas to your colours do you make a pencil sketch or a mental sketch?'

'Both,' he had replied.

Imroz was once asked if he had any similarity with the American painter Ivan Albright who had worked on one painting for twenty years.

He laughed and replied, 'I have painted a woman for the past thirty years. I was able to draw her physical features but it took me thirty long years to portray her mental being on canvas. I have been able to complete the painting this year. It is a painting of one line which appears like an instrument. It is a painting of an imaginary process, evolution of a mental construct as well as an instrument.'

Imroz has sprinkled his colours on the doors, walls and windows of his house in such a way that with the rays of the morning sun different colours are spread out all over the floor. Basu Bhattacharya, the famous film director, was so impressed by this display of colours that he desired to feature them in one of his movies.

In Amrita–Imroz's house, there is a window from where the summer's sharp sunlight enters. To restrict the bright sunlight, Imroz could have put curtains but he does not like them. So he ordered bamboo blinds, but they did not work.

Then he painted a picture of an earthen pot and wrote a few lines of Amrita's poem:

Uth apne ghare chon
Paani da kaul de
Dho lavangee baith ke
Ravaan de hadse
(Give me a cup full of water from your pitcher with which I will wash away the calamities of the way.)

When Amrita asked him, 'Is it Sohni's pitcher?' Imroz replied, 'No, it is yours.' (Sohni was the heroine of the love-legend *Sohni-Mahiwal*, who died while using an unbaked pitcher to cross the river to meet her lover.)

Imroz has decorated their house with his poem-paintings. There is a special rhythm in the beauty of his words, which can be called beat-of-the-art—its vibrations mix with the vibrations of pure consciousness and the power of art becomes its glory.

Imroz has painted lines such as *'Hajjis go to Mecca, we to Takht Haazaare'*. This is a quotation from a famous Sufi poet of Punjab who says in his poem that physical love and divine love mingle with each other like water, so there is no dividing line. For divine love, Mecca is the highest place of worship whereas Takhat Haazaare, the birth place of Ranjha, hero of the love-legend *Heer–Ranjha,* is the place of worship for lovers.

Imroz has not taken the words of this line in the physical sense but has painted the glance of a lover that turns an ordinary village into a place of worship. This glance is like a feather with a desire to fly to the place of worship and is a flight of the external physical self to the finer inner self.

Amrita had once commented on a Punjabi folk song which contains the lines :

Dharti noo kali karade ve
Nachangee saari raat.
(Paint the earth silver, I will dance the whole night.)

These simple lines reveal the kind of beauty which had not been bestowed on this earth so far. Words like *kali karade* contain in them a promise of the biggest revolution, which will wash away all the sins, injustice and oppression from the face of the earth. The promise of *Nachangee sari raat,* is the promise to live life to its fullest. It is an intense amalgam of hope, goodwill and a deep desire for universal well-being which Imroz has expressed through his paintings.

Faqira Aape Allah Ho is yet another line which Imroz has used in his paintings. It is a Sufi expression filled with the timeless desire to become many from one and one from many.

Imroz's painting of a large bird flying in the sky with a woman's body enfolded in its feathers, can be interpreted in many ways. Maybe it is the desire of the self to evolve from the gross self to the subtle self and to soar in the sky. Imroz feels that every creative desire is a desire to evolve.

Amrita once narrated this story: 'A friend of Kahlil Gibran mentioned to him that he wanted to compile his articles which he had written for various Arabic papers and magazines in his column 'A Tear and a Smile.' Kahlil replied: 'My past writings have been the expressions of my innocent youth. They are now dead and buried in the graveyard of my past dreams. Do you want to pick up the bones? Do whatever you please but do not forget that their souls have taken birth again in new beings.'

In this context Amrita remarked: 'That was perhaps a natural desire to mature from that innocence to maturity. The desire for evolution in Imroz's life did not come due to an instance in his life, it has been a continuous process.'

Imroz's painting *Ik Hasina* is another amazing painting. He has very creatively shown a lady's back, displaying all her beauty, charm and grace. Behind her is a dust storm in shades of green. This painting often sets Amrita thinking. She believes this must be Eve in the Garden of Eden, leaving behind her the garden and the greenery. Imroz's painting of Sai Bulleshah has a portrayal of regal mendicancy. Sai's eyes seem to have turned on himself after seeing the world. There is a thin cloth covering the intoxication of the inner self over which sadness is spread. People are returning from the location where the temples and mosques are being constructed, but with sad and collapsing hearts. Pain lies in being a Hindu, a Muslim, or anything else. But to discover oneself in being no one is the theme of the painting.

Another painting by Imroz, *Khuda di Pana,* depicting Hazrat Tahira, creates an ecstatic frenzy—a frenzy that could be seen in Tahira herself. When the sultan of that time offered Tahira his palace and the status of his wife, Tahira replied:

The rule of this land for you
The life of a mendicant for me

If that is better, then for you
If this is less then for me.

There are two paintings. In one, her face is covered with a very thin curtain and in the second, she is watching, at the time of her murder, her own death from a distance of four steps. Imroz has a magical way with colours. He has exquisitely painted Tahira's chiselled features and the fervour of mendicancy on her face.

In contrast, Imroz's painting of Gautam Buddha is unique, in the sense that the figure does not face the viewer, so one cannot see his features. Only his back, his neck and his head are visible amidst a haze. Perhaps this honours Buddha's desire not to be painted or portrayed in sculptures.

That day, I was left wondering about the similarities and contrasts in the life of two emotionally strong, creative individuals—Amrita and Imroz.

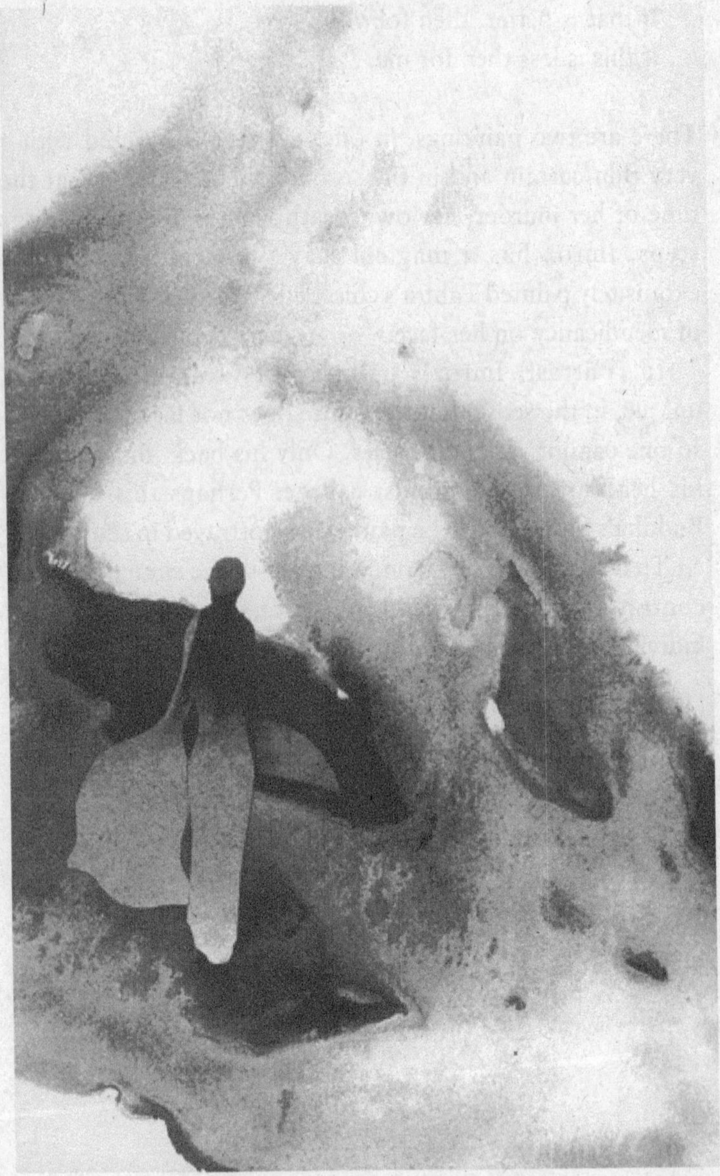

Twenty-five

Amrita's health was deteriorating every day. When I went to see her she spoke of a poem, on Imroz, which she had written. She was reading the lines very slowly and softly. When she could not read loud enough for me to hear she gave the poem to me to read.

Main tenu pher milaangee
Kithe kis tarah, pata nahi
Shayad teri takhyal dee chinag ban ke
Tere canvas te utrangee
Jaan khore tere canvas de utte
Ik rahasmayee lakeer ban ke
Khamosh tenu takdi ravangee
Jaan khore suraj di law ban ke
Tere rangan vich ghulaan gi
Tenu pher milaangee

(I will meet you again
Where, how, when

I know not
I will meet you again
As a spark of your imagination
I will fall on your canvas
I will gaze at you, in silence
As a mysterious line on your canvas
I will get dissolved as a beam of sunlight
Into the colours of your canvas
I will meet you again)

Jaan khore ik chashma bani howangi
Te jiven jhharnea da pani urhda
Mein paani diyan boonda
Tere pinde te malangee
Te ik thandak jehi ban ke
Teri chhati naal lagaangee.

(To scour the water drops on your body
Soaring spring, I will become.
I will shower myself on you
Like a serene sprinkle)

Mein hoar kujh nahin jaandee
Par ena jaandee haan
Ke vakt jo vee karegaa
Eh jaanam mere naal turegaa.
Eh jism mukda hai
Taan sab kujh muk jaanda hai

Par cheetana de dhaage
Kayanati kana de hunde ne
Mai uhna kana nu chunagee
Te tenu pher milangee

(Unaware of the rest
But aware I am, that
Time will favour me.
I know when body perishes,
Every thing perishes
But picking those specks of existence
That make the thread of memory.
I will meet you again)

As I finished reading, after many moments of choked silence to clear tears from my eyes, I saw her eyes opening, as if from a deep meditation. There was silence for several moments. Then, looking slowly towards me, she softly said: 'Would you translate it for me?'

I nodded silently and holding her in my arms I said, 'Yes, I will.'

That day we did not exchange many words. The healing process was carried out in silence.

I drove back in a sombre mood, my mind empty . . .

Twenty-six

Khushwant Singh, the writer, used to invite Amrita and Imroz occasionally for small get-togethers at his residence. When they started to avoid his invitations, he called Amrita and asked: 'Why don't you socialize? What do you both keep doing at home the whole day?'

She only said, '*Gallan*'. Which means spending time talking to each other.

He asked, 'What do you talk about?' She just laughed.

No one will understand how Amrita and Imroz remain in communication with each other all the time. Sometimes through the use of words and sometimes without. I wondered if it was like the sages who meet each other but do not talk and yet communicate everything. Imroz and Amrita enjoy each other's 'being', their togetherness.

These days Amrita lies in deep slumber. She speaks in syllables, sometimes.

But for Imroz, she is there always, as alert as ever. He does not converse with her though, like earlier times. But he talks to her and about her in his poems. In his latest poem 'Sohni' he lovingly brings her favourite flowers to her even when she does not ask for them any more.

Not only her favourite flowers, he also brings her bundles of dupattas embroidered with phulkari. He places them all before her—to choose one. He admires her choice, when he writes:

Parso main Patiale san
Ik bazaar vich phulkari design diyan
Bare ranga vich chunniyan dikhiyan
Mainu ainiyan changiyan lagiaan
Mai saariyan hee chuck liyandian han . . .

Lai hun gund khol ke
Tun aap chun lei.

(I was in Patiala
Day before yesterday
In the market I saw
Colourful dupattas
Embroidered in phulkari design
So beautiful they were all
I bought them all for you.
Now you open the bundle
And choose the one you like.)

But Amrita is so unwell she cannot sit up to choose or acknowledge his gesture. He knows it, yet it does not deter him. He visits the bookshops. Brings her Kazan Zanis's book

of letters for her. To read first and then pass on to him. He reminisces about the books they have read together earlier. In his poem 'Sohni' he goes on to describe Amrita as Sohni, who crossed a mighty river of Punjab with the help of a pitcher to meet her lover. Amrita, he finds, has crossed the entire Punjab with her literary pen many times in the past half-century.

In his poem 'Alna Ghar' Imroz calls himself an open house:

A house without a door,
Without a lock,
With no strings of a relationship,
With no interference from law.
Where no question is asked
Where no conditions are laid down
He is an open house
Under the open sky

He knows Amrita knows how to fly and he also knows the direction of her flight. He offers his house to her which is as large as himself. It further enlarges when Amrita enters. He knows Amrita's flight, this time, is going to be the longest. Each straw of this house welcomed her always and will now also bid her farewell. About Amrita, Imroz says:

Writing she lives
For her, life writes.
Distributing fertility
She, a full flowing river
Flows unending
To be the sea
Towards the sea.

Once, when Amrita was very sick and in the hospital, I became very sentimental and I asked Imroz, 'What will you do when Amrita leaves you? She is so sick that she may not be there for long. Don't you get pangs of separation? She has been the focus of your life for so long, what will you do without her?'

He smiled and said, 'Pangs of separation? What separation? *Kithe jaaoogi Amrita? Aaine aithe hee rehna hai, mere kol, mere duaale, hamesha.* (Where will Amrita go? She has to live here, with me, around me, always.) We have been together for forty years. Who can take her away from me? Not even death. I have memories of her of the past forty years and maybe of more, which I don't remember. Who can take her away from me?'

I just gazed into space in silence.

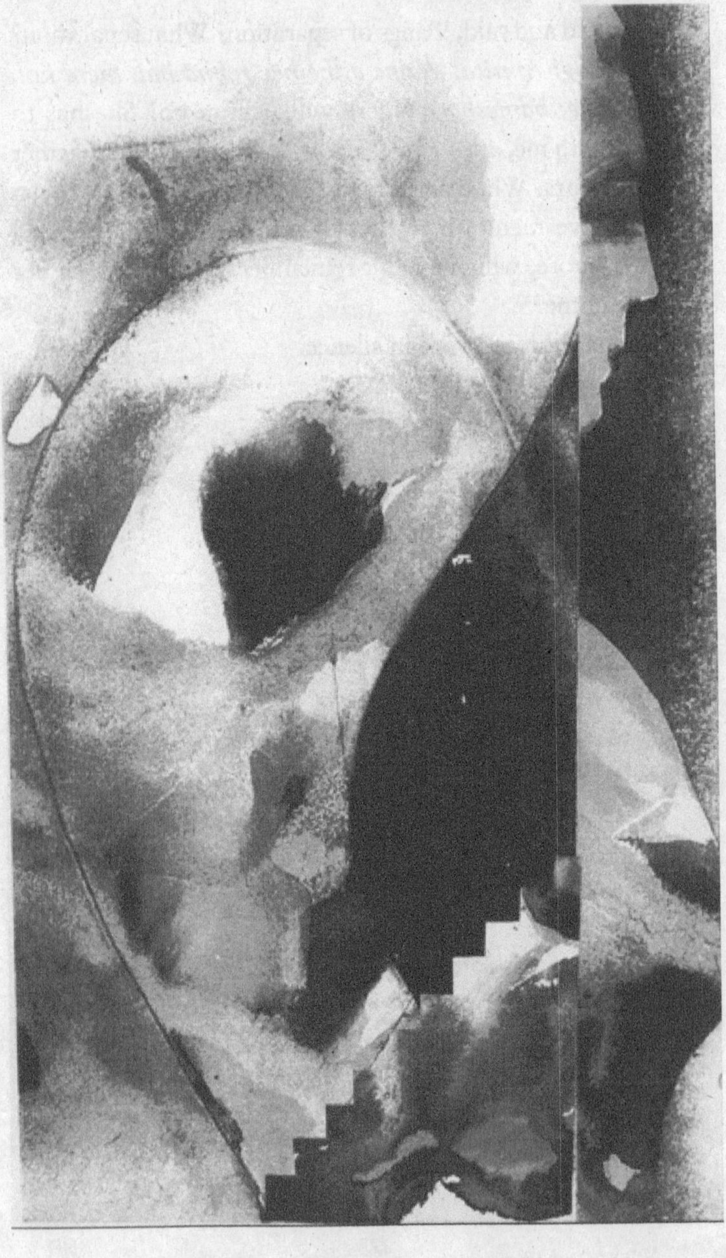

Twenty-seven

In the evening of 31 October, my telephone rang. I was a bit startled. Perhaps nature forewarns you, before an event occurs. As I picked up the phone, I heard Imroz's voice. He said 'Umaji' in a heavy voice. There was a long pause. 'Majaa is no more.'

I did not speak. In fact, I could not. Later I could only say '*Achchha main aati hoon*' (I will be there). To me it seemed as if I had heard this news before. Or perhaps I was waiting for it. We all knew that, now, only the news had to come. For all purposes—and for all of us, her friends and her literary world, she had already gone.

Towards the end, she had stopped speaking. She only stared. Sometimes, calling out to Imroz, she would say 'Ima, Ima'. She was not able to speak to him but by looking at him could convey to him what she wanted. Then everything would get done as she wished. Imroz would often say that her face communicated to him and her features spoke to him. He missed her voice, though.

A few days earlier he had written a poem on her features

and had recited it to me:

Kal raati sapne vich
Ik aurat dekhi
Jinoo mein pehle kadi nahi see vekheya
Par milde hee laggaya
Is bolde nain nakash wali noo
Pehle vee kite dekhya hoya see

(Seeing a woman in my dream last night
Whom I had not seen before
Looking at her eloquent features
I recognized her)

Two people, when in love, do not perhaps require to talk to each other. They read faces, read expressions—a pair of loving eyes communicates with another easily. I recollected Imroz's words: 'Sometimes beautiful thoughts take on beautiful bodies.'

When I reached her home I found that they had already taken the body to the cremation ground. At the end of the deserted cremation ground a few people were standing, silently staring at the burning pyre. Away from everybody, alone, standing in a corner, I spotted Imroz. Going close to him and touching his shoulder from behind, I muttered, 'Don't be sad.' Somehow I always felt that Imroz would become very sad after Amrita's death.

He turned, and looking at me, said, 'Uma, why be sad? What I could not do, Nature did.'

After a little pause he said, 'I could not free her from her physical pain. But, Nature has freed her.' After a while, with a mild smile on his face, he remarked, 'A soul broke away from her body, to become free again.'

I just kept looking at him. I was left speechless. Perhaps a person in love becomes a poet.

He not only writes poetry, he lives it. Knowing and understanding nature's ways, Imroz wrote the following lines soon after:

Kal tak zindgi koal ik rukh see
Zinda rukh.
Phulan phalan te mehkan naal bhareya
Te aj
Zindgi koal siraf ik zikar hai.
Zinda zikar.
Rukh jo hun beej ban gaya
Te beej
Hawawan nan ral ke ud gaya hai,
Pata nai kiss dharti dee talash vich

(Till yesterday
Life was like a tree,
A live tree
Laden with flowers, fruits and fragrance,
Today
Life has just a remembrance
A live remembrance

The tree has turned into a seed
And flown away with the winds
In search of new lands)

This reminded me of Amrita's own lines:

Keho jhehi is dee khushboi
phul moya par mehek na moi.
Kal honthan chon aandi pai see
Aj hunjuan chon andi pai ey
Bhalke yaadan chon avegee
Saari dharti vairagi hoi
Keho jehi is dee khushboi
Phul moya par mehak na moi

(Flower died, but not the fragrance
Fragrance emanated from the lips, yesterday
From the tears, today
From the memories, tomorrow
Nature's detachment depicted
Flower died, but not the fragrance)

We had all been used to seeing Amrita and Imroz in a series of meetings and partings—was this to be the last? Or, perhaps the next meeting will be an invisible one—a meeting of the souls.